Laws of the Landscape

BROOKINGS METRO SERIES

The Center on Urban and Metropolitan Policy of the Brookings Institution is integrating research and practical experience into a policy agenda for cities and metropolitan areas. By bringing fresh analyses and policy ideas to the public debate, the center hopes to inform key decisionmakers and civic leaders in ways that will spur meaningful change in our nation's communities.

As part of this effort, the Center on Urban and Metropolitan Policy has established the Brookings Metro Series to introduce new perspectives and policy thinking on current issues and attempt to lay the foundation for longer-term policy reforms. The series will examine both traditional urban issues, such as neighborhood assets and central city competitiveness, as well as larger metropolitan concerns, such as regional growth, development, and employment patterns. The Metro Series will consist of concise studies and collections of essays designed to appeal to a broad audience. While these studies are formally reviewed, some will not be verified like other research publications. As with all publications, the judgments, conclusions, and recommendations presented in the studies are solely those of the authors and should not be attributed to the trustees, officers, or other staff members of the institution.

BROOKINGS
METRO
SERIES

Laws of the Landscape

How Policies Shape Cities in Europe and America

Pietro S. Nivola

BROOKINGS INSTITUTION PRESS
Washington, D.C.

Library of Congress Cataloging-in-Publication data

Nivola, Pietro S.
    Laws of the landscape : how policies shape cities in Europe and America / Pietro S. Nivola.
        p.   cm.
    Includes bibliographical references and index.

    ISBN 0815760817 (alk. paper)
        1. Cities and towns—United States—Growth.   2. Urbanization—United States.   3. Suburbs—United States.   4. Cities and towns—Europe—Growth.   5. Urbanization-Europe.   I. Title.
    HT384.U5 N58 1999   98-58140
    307.76'0973-dc21   CIP

Digital printing
Manufactured in the United Sates of America

The paper used in this publication meets the minimum requirements of the American National Standard for Information Sciences—Permanence of Paper for Printed Library Materials, ANSI Z39.48-1984.

Typeset in New Baskerville and Myriad

Composition by R. Lynn Rivenbark
Macon, Georgia

Foreword

For the better part of this century, concerns have been raised about the relentless growth of suburbia in America's metropolitan regions. In part, suburban sprawl in the United States has reflected distinctive geographic, demographic, and economic circumstances. But a unique mix of public policies has also contributed to the phenomenon. Pietro S. Nivola raises important questions here: How has government influenced the pattern of urban development? Has the intervention been unsound or better than its alternatives? And if sprawl is to be controlled and core communities revitalized, what changes in policy would be desirable?

The book addresses these issues by comparing the dispersed layout of U.S. metropolitan areas with the relatively compact settlements in Europe. American and European cityscapes, Nivola argues, are often shaped by differences in what he calls "accidental urban policies"—how societies have organized everything from national tax and transportation systems, to housing strategies, agricultural subsidies, energy conservation efforts, protection of small businesses, and the distribution of local fiscal responsibilities.

In delineating possible reforms that could have beneficial consequences for the American metropolis and its central cities in particular, this study takes a hard look at the traditional U.S. urban programs, including downtown redevelopment projects, mass transit investments, "smart" growth controls, and metropolitan jurisdictional rearrangements. These exertions, the study concludes, have often been disappointing, partly because market forces have tugged in opposite directions, but also because the programs remain unsupported by the broader combination of policies prevailing in much of Europe. While most of the public agenda abroad cannot, and should not, be emulated here, Nivola finds that some general aspects are decidedly worth contemplating. They suggest ways that U.S. cities could gain, for example, from selective revisions of our tax structure, transportation budget, public housing program, and federal regulatory framework.

Readers of this book will come away with a better understanding of the causes and consequences of urban form on both sides of the Atlantic, and about what, if anything, U.S. policymakers can learn from foreign models.

This book launches the Brookings Institution Press's Brookings Metro Series. This new series, sponsored by the Brookings Center on Urban and Metropolitan Policy, is designed to spur fresh ways of thinking about America's cities and metropolitan areas and generate new policy responses to the challenges that remain. Upcoming publications in this series will address such issues as central-city competitiveness, metropolitan growth, regional collaborations, and asset building in inner-city neighborhoods. Nivola's comparative analysis of American and European cityscapes and policies demonstrates the type of new thinking to come from this series.

The author wishes to acknowledge the encouragement, comments, and assistance he received from Michael Armacost, Jennifer Bradley, Constance Beaumont, Gary Burtless, Flavio Delbono, Martha Derthick, William Dickens, John DiIulio Jr., Anthony Downs, William Gale, Deborah Gordon, Joseph Gyourko, Jacob Hacker, Laurel Imig, Bruce Katz, Robert Katzmann, John Kingdon, Joyce Ladner, Amy Liu, Thomas Mann, Carol O'Cleireacain, Janet Rothenberg Pack, Robert Reischauer, Heywood Sanders, Isabel Sawhill, Jon Shields, Peter Skerry, Brenda Szittya, Margaret Weir, and Clifford Winston. At the Brookings Institution Press, Kerry Kern edited the manuscript, Carlotta Ribar proofread the pages, and Sherry Smith provided the index.

The project was partially funded by grants from the George R. Gund Foundation, the Rockefeller Foundation, and the John D. and Catherine T. MacArthur Foundation.

The views expressed are the author's alone and should not be ascribed to the people or organizations whose assistance is acknowledged above or to the trustees, officers, and other staff members of the Brookings Institution.

MICHAEL H. ARMACOST
President

March 1999
Washington, D.C.

In honor of three teachers

Edward C. Banfield
Antonio Cederna
James Q. Wilson

Contents

Laws of the
Landscape

CHAPTER ONE

Introduction

The planning commission of America's largest city issues an alarm. In a thick report on the transformation of the metropolis, the commission laments the region's pattern of settlement on "urban fringes." Development has "proceeded indiscriminately," extending "into areas which are predominantly rural in character." The "urban growth outside the city" is also taking "forms that do not harmonize with and may be injurious to the central community."[1]

This sounds a lot like today's New Urbanists describing the ills of sprawl—but the words are those of the New York Regional Plan of 1929.[2] Concern about the relentless expansion of suburbs in the United States, and about the consequences for the countryside and core communities, is an old story. Suburban growth, after all, has been a secular trend spanning the century. While that hardly makes the issue less pertinent now, it raises at least three basic questions. First, has suburbanization been induced by the interventions of government, not just by long-standing and irreversible market forces? Second, how much of the government intervention has been undesirable? Finally, what changes in public policies make sense at this late date?

This book will address these matters by viewing the American cityscape from a comparative perspective. The outward movement of people and jobs in metropolitan areas has been not only a phenomenon of long duration but one common worldwide. The reason is not complicated. Urban populations and commercial activities can only grow in four directions: *in* (by crowding), *up* (as in Manhattan's skyscrapers), *down* (as in Tokyo's 700 subterranean mah-jongg parlors), and *out* (as on the peripheries of cities nearly everywhere except Gibraltar). Growth is likely to follow the last of these paths overwhelmingly, particularly in advanced countries endowed with abundant usable territory. The United States is obviously one of these countries, but so are some others. To accommodate the pressure of growth the Australian city of Adelaide expanded more between 1939 and 1965 than it had in the previous one hundred years.[3] Sydney and Melbourne each grew to cover an area larger than London, a mega-city with four times as many people but encircled by a comparatively limited supply of land available for development.[4]

Nonetheless, nowhere in the industrial world is suburban settlement more extensive than in the United States. In 1950 about one-quarter of the U.S. population lived in suburbia. Today, more than half does.[5] Meanwhile, most U.S. city centers have lost inhabitants, often by the hundreds of thousands.[6] The reach of this reconfiguration, especially in the decades following the second world war, suggests that some unusual forces have been at work. How unusual becomes apparent only when the American experience is compared with conditions elsewhere.

Inasmuch as the form of the modern American metropolis has been shaped by policies, not just Mother Nature, redirecting some of them might still make a difference. To gain a realistic sense of the prospects, however, requires at a minimum taking the full measure of what is distinctive about this country's public agenda and just how much of it Americans would be willing to trade for various foreign models. As we shall see, such an assessment leads perforce beyond cross-national contrasts in traditional urban programs such as housing and transportation subsidies, inner-city redevelopment projects, "wars" on inner-city poverty, and so on. Also at issue are fundamental differences in the ways societies have organized everything from their national tax systems and local fiscal responsibilities to energy conservation efforts, agricultural subventions, and insulation from the competitive heat of international commerce. These differing choices might be called accidental urban policies, for their effects on the design of cities are commonly unrecognized, even if possibly profound.

CHAPTER TWO

Big and Turbulent

The United States, Antoine de Saint Exupéry once reminded his fellow Frenchmen, is not just a country but a continent. Into its 3,540,000 square miles one could fit the entire land mass of western and eastern Europe (excluding only Russia), throw in Japan, and still have more than a million square miles left. Inhabiting this continental nation are 268 million persons, or 40 percent of the combined populations of Europe and Japan, which total 672 million.[1] With fewer people and so much room to roam, densities in U.S. cities have remained thin in comparison with those in Europe or Japan.[2] Even New York, our most dense major city, has roughly one-third the number of persons per square mile of Frankfurt and one-fifth the persons per square mile of Tokyo.[3]

Americans, perhaps with excessive abandon, continue to take advantage of their spacious environs. Between 1982 and 1992 the state of Arizona sacrificed 49,280 acres a year to urban development. Even if this rapid rate were to continue unchecked well into the next millennium, however, Arizona's urbanized acreage in the year 2020 would remain under 2 percent of the state's overall surface.[4] One can debate how "sustainable" that fraction will be, but clearly one cannot argue that vacant land in places like Arizona is a comparatively scarce commodity to be husbanded the way it is in, say, the Netherlands. Space is one of America's plentiful resources, along with other geographic assets such as bountiful rivers, 12,383 miles of coastline, and huge reserves of natural gas.[5] To expect that space should be utilized as parsimoniously here as in countries with precious little of it is no different than suggesting we should emulate them by transporting more goods on trucks instead of river barges and coastal freighters or rely even more on oil imports and nuclear power plants than on gas-fired furnaces and generators. When allocating resources, each nation naturally puts its particular comparative advantages to extensive use.

space as comparative advantage?

Demographics

The expansive utilization of urban land in the United States reflects not only the simple fact that there is plenty of it to consume, but also the extraordinary pace of U.S. postwar population growth compared to that of most other industrial countries. From 1950 through 1996 the United States added more than 113 million people, an increase of approximately 74 percent.[6] Japan added some 42 million, an increase of 50 percent. Germany gained 14 million and Italy gained less than 10 million, both representing increases of about 20 percent over the forty-six year period. The population of the United Kingdom increased by less than 15 percent, from 50 million to slightly above 57 million. It is not surprising that British cities were able to absorb in almost half a century their relatively small number of new inhabitants without sprawling well beyond existing city limits (although even there the surrounding greenbelts are now threatened by developers).[7] It would have been surprising, indeed, if America—with more than fifteen times the growth of Britain—had been able, or inclined, to contain its demographic surge within similar limits.

With a faster rate of growth, the U.S. population has also had a different age profile. Birth rates in major European countries in 1997 ranged from 9.5 births per 1,000 persons (Germany) to

12.8 births per 1,000 (the United Kingdom).[8] The U.S. level in 1997 was 14.6. While only 14.8 percent and 16 percent of the populations of Italy and Germany, respectively, are under fifteen years of age, almost 22 percent of Americans are that young. Households with young children tend to seek suburban dwellings, if for no other reason than to gain residential space.

Metropolitan areas expand by way of in-migration as well as natural increases. Several urban regions of Europe have faced a significant influx, even as population in their countries as a whole grew modestly. Cities in the industrial north of Italy have taken in large numbers of migrants from the south. Still, migration within European countries, not to mention between them, pales in contrast to the degree of interregional mobility in the United States. During certain years in the early 1980s, for example, northern Italy acquired as many as 55,000 migrants annually from other parts of the country.[9] Meanwhile, during the first half of that decade, the American West netted 130,000 migrants a year, the South 380,000 a year.[10] With more than 90 percent of the flow pouring into these regions' urban areas, several experienced explosive growth. By the mid-1990s towns like Phoenix had become major agglomerations, sometimes spreading a million or more residents over hundreds of square miles.[11]

In magnitude, nothing remotely comparable to this has happened to European cities in recent memory, even though the outskirts of places like Milan or Turin have had to house substantial numbers of newcomers. The explanation is straightforward. Individually, no country in Europe comes close, geographically or demographically, to the size of the United States. So even where the absolute volumes of European intracountry migration might appear large by internal standards, they are small in comparison with the U.S. aggregate. In Exupéry's terms, mobility in Europe remains circumscribed by some forty national borders and the lack of a common language, whereas Americans move freely across a continent. Movements of population on the U.S. scale have obvious implications for their destinations: the settlements swell and quickly spill outward onto vacant tracts.

Violence

In any given year some 43 million Americans change their place of residence. This phenomenal mobility has its virtues, but the resulting destabilization of communities is not one of them.[12] The demolition of civic cohesion, shared values, and trust in many neighborhoods is associated with higher levels of violent crime.[13] Although levels of serious crime in the United States have fluctuated considerably over the past seventy-five years, even at their lowest point they far exceeded the rates of other leading democracies.[14] The root causes of why, in a typical year, a person is ten times more likely to be murdered in America than in Japan, seven times more likely to be raped than in France, or almost four times more likely to be robbed at gun point than in the United Kingdom remain a mystery.

Mysterious or not, two things are known. First, an exceptional propensity for criminal violence is not a novel American distinction. The U.S. homicide rate in 1993, for example, was slightly lower than the level sixty years earlier. Second, rates of personal victimization, including murder, rape, assault, robbery, and personal theft, typically tend to be sharply higher within U.S. central cities than in their surroundings.[15]

There is a reasonably clear connection between urban crime rates and the flight of households and businesses to suburbs. A city nets a loss of one resident for every additional crime committed within it.[16] Attitudinal surveys have regularly ranked public safety as a leading concern in the selection of residential locations.[17] In 1992, when New Yorkers were asked to name "the most important reason" for moving out of the city, the most frequent answer was "crime, lack of safety" (47.2 percent).[18] All other reasons—including "high cost of living" (9.3 percent) and "not enough affordable housing" (5.3 percent)—lagged far behind. Similarly, businessmen frequently identify crime as the major impediment to locating in the inner city.[19] In sum, a society that supplies so little security for its frightened city dwellers, and so much opportunity for most of them to exit, abets a tendency to hollow out the cores of many metropolitan areas, scattering a lot of their jobs and people.

The Churning Pot

Another enduring determinant of urban spatial structure in the United States has been the country's ethnic, racial, and religious heterogeneity. This consideration is too often given a misleading or simplistic spin—as when the exodus to suburbs gets imputed almost exclusively to the "racial attitudes" of whites. Yet, there is no question that race and ethnicity have long played a formative role in the evolution of urban America, a role with few parallels abroad. No other western country has had so large and distinct a racial minority heavily concentrated in cities. That, however, is but one of the marked differences.

In Australia and Canada foreign-born residents have represented an impressive proportion of the population, but in absolute terms the *combined* number of foreign-born in these two countries is only 40 percent of the U.S. total. Japan is for all intents and purposes a homogeneous culture; merely 1.1 percent of its residents are not ethnic Japanese.[20] The small minority primarily consists of ethnic Koreans, many of whom have resided in Japan for generations without Japanese citizenship. A seemingly large proportion of Germany's population is reported to be "foreign" (8.5 percent in 1993), but Germany (like Japan) continues to count the native-born descendants of foreign ancestors as aliens, even after several generations. As of 1993 less than 2 percent of the population of Italy had other national origins. In France, where immigrants can be naturalized, the influx reached 6.3 percent by 1995—still not close to the U.S. level, which reached almost 10 percent by 1997.[21] A total of approximately 15 million persons of foreign origin were residing in Japan, France, Germany, Italy, Spain, and the United Kingdom in 1993; that same year close to 20 million bona fide foreigners were living in America.

Assimilating this country's massive waves of diverse groups has never been easy. While tortured relations between whites and blacks scar much of U.S. history, there have been other severe and savage ethnocentric collisions. Nativist attacks on various immigrant nationalities in the nineteenth century were so common and widespread that no historian has tried to track them all.[22] Here, for a general sense of what was going on, is a sampling of a few incidents. Tempestuous anti-Catholic riots, with many casualties, rocked Philadelphia, Cincinnati, and Boston in the 1840s and 1850s. In 1861 Irish regiments of the Union army, on their way to the front from New York and Boston, were stoned passing through Baltimore. A mob in San Francisco murdered twenty-one Chinese during a riot in 1877. In Chicago in 1886 five German immigrants were arbitrarily arrested and sentenced to death. Six Italians were lynched in southern Colorado in 1891 and fourteen more in Louisiana the following year.[23] A pogrom in a New Jersey mill town in 1891 sent most of its Jewish inhabitants fleeing for their lives. Twenty-one Polish and Hungarian coal miners were massacred in Hazelton, Pennsylvania, in 1897.

Nevertheless, the genius of the American republic has been its capacity to absorb the successive shocks of ethnic diversity. One of the cultural shock absorbers has been the promise of upward social mobility for virtually all groups, including African Americans, but another has been *physical* mobility, facilitated by ample space and the swift diffusion of formidable technologies.[24] During the nineteenth century, railroads plunged into the frontier, delivering millions to the western territories. The conquest was not pretty; entire Native American peoples in its path were displaced or annihilated. But arguably, without the western expansion, the ethnic and racial caldron in the teeming cities of the East would have boiled over even more violently than it did. In the twentieth century, the free-wheeling migration of tens of millions of city folk to suburbs was a similarly useful escape valve. It put some breathing room between groups that earlier had been stuffed into cities cheek-by-jowl.

One may wonder whether nations that have lacked this spatial buffer, or that prefer to compress their urban populations into much closer physical proximity, could have kept a lid on urban social pressures comparable in duration and intensity to those withstood historically in America. Plainly stated, a good deal of sprawl in this country may be a necessary complement to its extreme multiculturalism.[25]

Technological Turmoil

Before turning to less deterministic factors in the layout of U.S. metropolitan areas, a final point bears emphasis. The introduction of new technologies upended the old physical plants of cities all over the industrial word, but nowhere as early and tumultuously as in the United States. Even when pivotal industrial inventions originated elsewhere, they were embraced rapidly and on a broad scale in America. As early as the 1880s, the extension of street railways and trolleys from the centers of older cities was turning outlying areas into new residential subdivisions. This is how largely uninhabited districts south of Boston, such as Roxbury and Dorchester, were opened to development.[26] The percentage of population that gained access to the fringes of Philadelphia in the latter part of the nineteenth century actually approximated the percentage for the first half of the twentieth.

In 1904 there were barely 700 trucks on the roads of the United States. Great Britain, the birthplace of the industrial revolution, had almost thirteen times as many.[27] Fourteen years later there were 605,000 trucks operating in America; Britain was a distant second with 83,000. The impact of the truck was enormous. The advent of linear-flow industrial plants, beginning with Henry Ford's assembly line in 1913, had greatly increased the space requirements of manufacturing firms. Cramped inner-city sites had to be abandoned for large and inexpensive suburban tracts. Trucks made the transition possible. They enabled raw materials and finished products to be transported from more points in an urban region, detaching factories from their traditional adjacency to downtown harbors and rail depots. The new industrial nodes, in turn, attracted secondary and tertiary growth, as worker housing and related services collected around them.

Automobiles quickly accelerated the dispersion. Again, the impetus came much earlier in America than elsewhere. On the eve of the first world war, British auto manufacturers were assembling 34,000 cars a year in the fashion of a craft industry. But Ford Motor Company's streamlined plants cranked out 784,800 cars in 1916.[28] So affordable were the Fords that by the mid-1920s about

56 percent of all families owned an automobile. No European country attained anything like that level of automobile ownership until well after the second world war.[29] America's motorized multitudes were able to commute between suburban residences and workplaces many decades before this type of human ecology was conceivable in almost any other advanced nation.

While the automobile has come to be considered the prime mover of America's "edge cities," the role of other, more recent technical advances should not be underestimated. It is hard to imagine how Houston, Dallas, Phoenix, and Miami could have grown as much as they did without the existence of air conditioning. Breathtaking progress in telecommunications and information technology has enhanced the locational flexibility of firms, service suppliers, and customers. Communication has become less a function of distance. In many industries, the need for ready access to dense pools of clerical workers, proximity to urban markets, and face-to-face contact keeps diminishing.

U.S. cities saw the onset of almost every one of these changes well ahead of most cities overseas. Consequently, much of the momentum of urban decentralization in this country has been path dependent: technological innovations helped chart an early course that has determined, and been amplified by, subsequent events.

The Not-So-Invisible Hand

Fundamental circumstances, such as distinctive geographic, demographic, and technological characteristics, as well as rapidly rising incomes, go a long way toward explaining the American style of metropolitan development. But they do not explain all of it.[1] Actions of government, sometimes intentionally, often not, have supplied additional stimulus for the unbounded extension of suburbia. *Subsidization*

Perhaps the simplest way to test this inference is to notice the limited part played by population increases—the most basic natural force behind all metropolitan growth—in urban regions like New York, Chicago, or Cleveland in recent decades.[2] Each of these is a place where population has either grown modestly or not at all, yet the consumption of land has continued to be voracious. From 1970 to 1990, the New York region's population grew by 8 percent, while the region's urbanized land increased by 65 percent. The Chicago area's population rose by only 4 percent during these twenty years, but that region's built-up land increased 46 percent. Cleveland's population actually declined by 8 percent, yet the metropolis expanded geographically by 33 percent. It is hard to understand patterns like these without factoring in the inducement from public policies.

Laying Asphalt

How much government intervention formed, rather than followed, new suburbs is not always easy to tell. Some policy choices clearly provided preconditions. Of these decisions, surely none has left a greater imprint than has the nation's legendary devotion to building roads. It is hard to picture how motor vehicles—the machines that here more than anywhere propelled households and businesses out of the old cities—could have let loose so vast a mass mobilization without a sustained public investment in highways. That investment is usually thought to have begun in earnest in 1956 when the federal government began paving a network that would eventually link together distant cities. In fact, the program launched that year was not the first significant promotion of road construction. State governments, with federal assistance, had initiated their own major projects decades earlier. Nor was the United States the only industrial country to envision in the immediate postwar period an integrated nationwide system of highways. France, for example, began building a national system at about the same time.

At least two features have distinguished the U.S. commitment. One was the installation of self-perpetuating mechanisms to finance it. After 1956 a semiautonomous federal trust fund, continually replenished by specially designated tax collections, started pouring a stream of revenue into construction projects. As early as 1934, however, Congress had asked as a condition for receipt of highway grants-in-aid that state governments dedicate even the proceeds from their own turnpike tolls exclusively to the improvement of roads. (Earlier still, most state constitutions had earmarked tolls and fuel taxes in this restrictive fashion.) In almost all other industrial countries, by contrast, highway plans have always been supported out of general revenue, thereby forcing these public works to compete with other priorities in national budgets. The result in many cases abroad has been a comparatively "underfunded" infrastructure for automotive transport.

With a spare-no-expense approach to highway expansions, the size of the U.S. effort became unique. Great distances between cities or states in this country do not wholly account for the magnitude; U.S. interstate plans called for massive expenditures, not just on transcontinental facilities, but also on urban radial and circumferential arteries designed to enhance intra-metropolitan access. These local webs of roadways have sped the dispersal of jobs and housing within metropolitan areas.

So integral to the ascent of suburbs was America's exuberant road building that urbanists sometimes regard U.S. highway planners as a kind of wrecking crew, conspiring in the demise of central cities. What the critics sometimes forget is that, earlier in the century, the same cities were widely deemed overcrowded and clogged and that routing traffic out and around them would provide relief. To decongest their downtowns, city officials, merchants, and housing experts—not just the developers of suburban subdivisions and shopping centers—pleaded for highway bypasses. In the 1950s, moreover, cold war fears were more than a pretext for the National System of Interstate and Defense Highways (as the federal road program was formally called). The thinking at the time was that an extensive alternative to rail transport would genuinely enhance national security, as would some deliberate deconcentration of housing and industry from vulnerable urban centers.[3] The highways, in short, were thought to *save* the cities, not just enlarge suburbia at their expense.

Public Transportation

Contrary to a widely held misperception, U.S. funding of public transit has not languished. Adjusted for inflation, the federal government has invested more than $80 billion in capital equipment alone since 1965.[4] State and local governments have expended at least that much of their own funds since 1982.[5] Hundreds of miles of new rail transit lines have been laid in Atlanta, Miami, Baltimore, Buffalo, Detroit, Los Angeles, San Francisco, Washington, D.C., and other cities around the country. With most urban transit systems running massive deficits every year, their operating expenses have been subsidized by at least another $130 billion cumulatively.[6]

Figure 3-1. *U.S. Expenditures for Transportation, All Levels of Government,
1977–95*

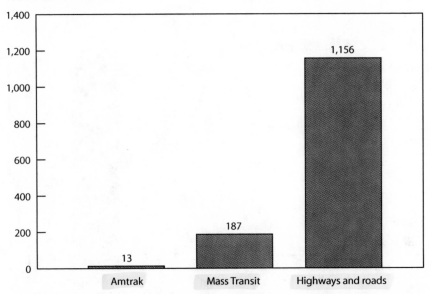

In billions of dollars

Sources: Federal Highway Administration, *Highway Statistics Summary to 1996*, pp. IV-29–IV-38; American Public Transit Association, *Transit Fact Book, 1992*, pp. 51, 59, www.apta.com/pubs/stats; Amtrak, Amtrak Appropriations History 1971–98, unpublished data.

What counts, however, is not the absolute sum of this aid, enormous as it is, but the *distribution* of public expenditures among modes of transportation (see figure 3-1). Where, as in the United States, the share claimed by roads has dwarfed that of alternatives, it was not surprising to see an unrelenting increase in automobile travel and a steady slide in transit usage, however heavily subsidized. In 1945 transit accounted for approximately 35 percent of urban passenger miles traveled.[7] By 1994 the figure had dwindled to less than 3 percent—or roughly one-fifth the average in western Europe.[8]

The abandonment of public transportation is primarily a consequence of higher per capita incomes and low urban density. The clustered populations and workplaces of European and Japanese cities offer the critical mass needed to maintain comparatively high

Figure 3-2. *Government Expenditures for Transportation in France, Great Britain, and the United States, 1993*

In millions of dollars, using purchasing power parity

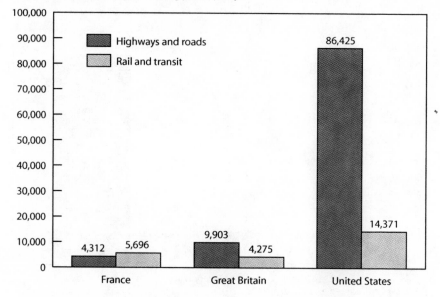

Sources: I.N.S.E.T., *Les Transports en 1995*, p. 164; Department of Transport, *Transport Statistics Great Britain*, 1995 ed., p. 29; Federal Highway Administration, *Highway Statistics Summary to 1996*, pp. IV-37, www.apta.com/pubs/stats; Amtrak, Amtrak Appropriations History 1971–98, unpublished data.

levels of transit ridership, whereas the decentralized urban conurbations of the United States are more efficiently served by automotive transportation. But to some degree, density is determined by the mix of transportation policies. If, early on, American planners had followed, say, the British or French budgetary practice of allocating between 40 and 60 percent of their transportation outlays to passenger railroads and mass transit systems instead of highways, many U.S. cities quite probably would be more compact today (see figure 3-2).[9]

Fuel Pricing

Many U.S. cities might be even more compact if, as in most of Europe, they had supplied not only fewer metropolitan freeways along which to scatter development but a second potent incentive to reside closer to transit services: namely, European-style fuel prices.

It is important to be precise on this question. A number of antagonists of America's "love affair" with the automobile insist that its operating costs are being grossly subsidized. One study, published in 1992, calculated the annual subsidy at no less than $300 billion.[10] To stop this supposed free ride, motorists presumably ought to pay user fees and gasoline taxes many times their current levels. Current user charges, such studies claim, cover only about 60 percent of the tens of billions of dollars the federal and state governments spend each year building, improving, and repairing roads. Taxpayers at large pay for the rest.

The premises of calculations like these are not entirely convincing. For one thing, they chalk up as part of the "subsidy" to American motorists unavoidable public expenditures, such as the annual expense of maintaining a U.S. military presence in the Persian Gulf. (U.S. armed forces would need to defend the Gulf regardless of how much or little Americans drive their cars.) For another, in a society where virtually every household owns at least one vehicle, a distinction between highway users and general taxpayers seems somewhat artificial. Almost everybody in the United States utilizes highway facilities and services and gets taxed for this utilization through levies of one kind or another.[11] Further, some of the costs paid by operators of motor vehicles in the United States may actually be too high, not too low. Rampant liability litigation associated with accidents, for example, may be inflating automobile insurance premiums by almost $50 billion a year.[12]

Nevertheless, this much is certain: Compared to every other industrial country, the cost of driving in the United States is a bargain, thanks largely to the minimal average U.S. tax rate on automotive fuel (see figure 3-3). Bargain-basement fuel helps explain why American consumers buy more and bigger vehicles and use them much more intensively than European, let alone Japanese, consumers do (see figure 3-4).

Naturally, the vehicle mileage logged by U.S. drivers is also a function of the country's size—but less so than commonly assumed.

Figure 3-3. *Average Price per Gallon for Unleaded Gasoline*

In 1996 dollars

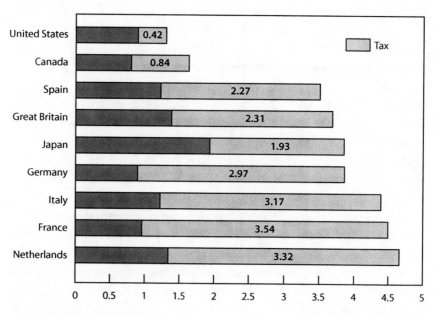

Source: *Washington Post,* May 11, 1996, p. A21.

Two-thirds of all vehicle miles traveled in the United States are on urban roads, not open plains.[13] Ninety percent of the trips are fewer than ten miles in length. This appears to be virtually the same as or shorter than the average length of trips in some other countries, including Germany and Britain. As one expert observes, the main difference between the Europeans and Americans is not that the latter have much farther to go or that they generally go farther; instead, the difference is that Americans drive more frequently, whereas Europeans more often stay put, walk, or use other modes of transportation.[14] Up to a point, what makes this distinction inevitable is the predominance in the United States of a comparatively diffuse pattern of metropolitan growth. But what permits the U.S. diffusion to be viable in the first place is, in part, low-cost energy, which has fueled the relatively unrestrained use of vehicles.

Figure 3-4. *Comparison of Passenger Vehicle Miles Traveled per Capita,*
1976–91

Thousands of passenger vehicle miles

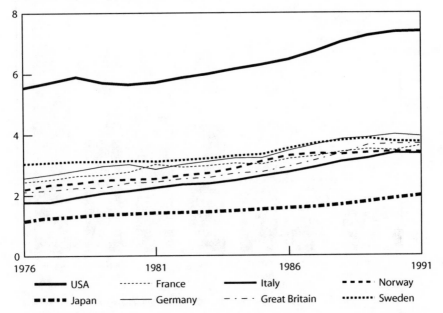

Sources: Data drawn from Lee Schipper and others, "Mind the Gap: The Vicious Circle of Measuring Automobile Fuel Use," *Energy Policy*, vol. 21 (December 1993), p. 1182; Lee Schipper and others, "Fuel Prices and Economy: Factors Affecting Land Travel," *Transport Policy*, vol. 1, no. 1 (1993), pp. 6–20; and more recent data provided by Lawrence Berkeley Laboratory, Berkeley, Calif.

Energy Policies

Transportation is not the only sector of the American economy powered by relatively inexpensive energy. The costs of almost everything else, from heating buildings to running electrical appliances, has tended to be cheaper in the United States than in other industrial nations (see figure 3-5). Much as economical travel by automobile has been instrumental to suburban growth, cut-rate furnace fuels and electricity have enhanced the marketability of the typical U.S. suburban subdivision, with its relatively large detached structures. Per kilowatt hour and per square meter of dwelling

Figure 3-5. *International Comparison of Energy Prices for Households*

In 1993 dollars/toe[a]

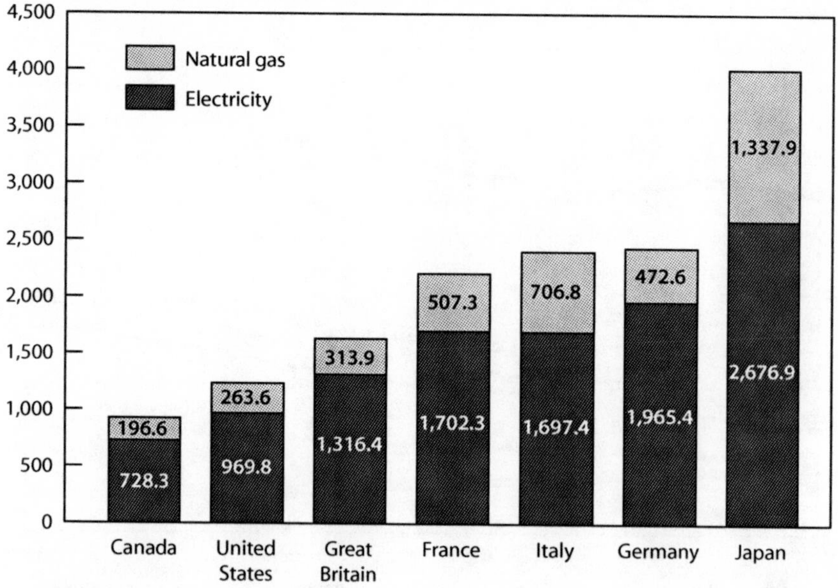

Source: International Energy Agency, *Energy Prices and Taxes: Second Quarter 1995* (Paris: IEA/OECD, 1995), pp. 269, 272.
a. toe = 10[7] kilocalorie.

space, European and Japanese consumers face utility bills far costlier than the norm in the United States. The expense of heating the equivalent of an average U.S. suburban home and of operating the large home appliances (such as refrigerators and freezers) that substitute for neighborhood shops in many American residential communities would be daunting to most households in large parts of Europe and in Japan.

Most of the energy bonanza that Americans have traditionally enjoyed derives from the country's natural endowments, not its policy prescriptions. As noted earlier, the United States has been blessed with abundant reserves of natural gas. U.S. deposits of coal are even more impressive. Vast amounts of hydroelectric power are generated in some regions. U.S. oilfields yield more petroleum each year than those of any other producer in the world except Saudi Arabia.[15] It would be peculiar if a nation so fortunate did not unleash the full force of market demand on this rich supply of resources.

But market forces have not always been the only determinant of energy consumption in American society. At key junctures a meddlesome government has brought additional influence to bear.[16] Recall that the price of the nation's premier heating fuel, natural gas, was regulated by federal authorities for decades (technically from 1954 until 1989). For at least some of that period, the policy of the regulators was to depress prices below their true marginal cost, thereby artificially stimulating demand. In the 1970s similar price controls on domestic crude oil had much the same effect. Meanwhile, the federal and state commissions that designed rate structures for electricity were frequently pricing this form of energy, too, below its would-be marginal price.[17]

The United States was not the only country that sought to shield consumers from rising energy prices, particularly in the 1970s and early 1980s. Canada, for example, experimented with even stiffer controls on the prices of oil and gas, and some European governments tried to restrain electric rates. But only nations that were largely self-sufficient in energy production, like the United States and Canada, could claim any measure of success in their dubious social objective of forcing prices down to "affordable" levels. Countries such as Japan or Italy that were wholly at the mercy of world markets for their supplies of fossil fuels had little choice but to leave consumers fully exposed to global price pressures.

The result in venues like Japan and most European countries was that traditional constraints on energy-intensive luxuries such as spacious housing and lavish reliance on automobiles drew tighter as energy prices soared in the 1970s. At times, U.S. consumers were also inconvenienced, but the basic consumption habits that have consistently sustained the American suburban habitat were scarcely reversed or even momentarily interrupted.

Housing Policies

The wave of rural migrants that flooded into American cities to man production plants during the second world war did not abate in the 1950s. Rapid economic growth continued to draw workers from the hinterlands, swelling an urban population that was also burgeoning from the postwar demobilization and baby boom. City housing stocks, already crowded, had to expand. The federal government responded in two ways. It funneled money into the cities to construct public housing projects, and it facilitated through mortgage insurance programs a building boom of middle-income housing on outlying land. — Increase home ownership

Both these steps helped induce an unprecedented burst of suburban development. Federal Housing Administration (FHA) and Veterans Administration mortgage guarantees accounted for as much as one-quarter of all the single-family homes built in the postwar period. The FHA's standard operating procedures, which favored lending for new construction over repairs of existing structures and instructed underwriters to exclude racially mixed neighborhoods deemed unstable, inevitably funneled loans to suburban locations.[18] At the same time, the locus of federally funded public housing increased the concentration of low-income households deep inside the cities, aggravating their social pathologies and fiscal burdens and ultimately giving more affluent citizens further reason to move out.[19]

Policies in much of Europe differed in several respects. Many European cities had been devastated by the war. Housing shortages were far more acute than in the United States. European governments faced an urgent need to rebuild the stock, not only for the poor but also for much of the middle class. Thus, a comparatively large share of households—commonly two to three times the U.S. percentage—found themselves in publicly funded housing.[20] To this day, directly subsidized units in many European cities contain a broader socioeconomic mix of residents than do the tightly means-tested projects managed by municipal housing authorities in the United States.

Examples abound. As stark as any has been the contrast between, say, the housing "estate" of La Courneuve near Paris and the notorious public housing complexes in the vicinity of Woodlawn, on the South Side of Chicago.[21] The latter have been racially segregated (virtually all black) and inhabited by households on public assistance. La Courneuve has been racially mixed (25 percent nonwhite). Most heads of its households have been fully employed, although the percentage has worsened in recent years amid France's alarmingly high rate of unemployment. The Chicago complexes have long constituted a ghetto, blighting a large swath of the city and chasing nearby residents away. La Courneuve may be changing, but for most of its existence it has been a place that average Parisians were not afraid to live in or near.[22]

In addition, decisions about tenancy and location have distinguished U.S. from prevalent European policies. While planners in the United States were relegating the poor to rental units in the inner cities and underwriting the spread of owner-occupied homes for better-off families in the suburbs, the Europeans extended mainly rental subsidies and often placed their government-sponsored apartment houses on the peripheries of cities. Almost one-quarter of all so-called council housing in London, for example, is located in "outer" London.[23] Although the heart of this metropolis has its share of grim projects and slums, they are not so dominant as to inspire nine thousand Londoners to desert the core of the English capital every year. (Nine thousand was the net average number of residents abandoning the capital of the United States each year from 1990 to 1996.)[24]

It is commonly assumed that in much of Europe the spatial distribution of "affordable" housing reflects only the raw power of central governments to impose their will on all localities, including those encircling major cities. Suburban communities in the United States, in contrast, are almost always at liberty to veto plans to accommodate low- or moderate-income families. In fact, the reality is not so simple. Even in Britain and France, both highly centralized unitary regimes, local authorities retain considerable discretion over the use of land. But subsidized housing has claimed a wider clientele there and so has tended to get a somewhat better reception in more locations. In part this is because the subsidies, instead of chiefly erecting edifices for the urban underclass, have long spanned a relatively broad spectrum of society.[25] In part, too, the fact that European housing programs were extensively supporting renters, not homeowners, played a part. By 1960 almost 62 percent of all U.S. households owned their own homes, a percentage unparalleled in European countries. Homeowners tend to be especially sensitive to the income and racial makeup of their communities, fearing that the introduction of mixed housing can "tip" property values.

To attract population and businesses back into America's older urban neighborhoods, or at least to slow the pace of exurban growth in the past half century, policymakers almost certainly would have had to change the socioeconomic composition of many central cities. Bluntly stated, many would have had to disperse their ghettos, distributing the inhabitants much more evenly among jurisdictions throughout metropolitan regions. What it would have taken to accomplish this feat is not entirely clear, but an early shift toward the promotion of mixed-income rental housing might have been essential, as would an ability to situate its poorest beneficiaries in a wider range of sites than the likes of Chicago's South Side. By and large, this was the orientation of the postwar housing strategies of various European countries. U.S. initiatives advancing mixed-income residence through the Department of Housing and Urban Development's rental assistance programs got a relatively late and limited start and have barely begun to penetrate the suburbs.[26]

Systems of Taxation

For decades Americans living in metropolitan areas have revealed a preference for owning their own homes, typically in the form of single-family structures on separate plots of land. The aspiration has been aided by the federal tax code's allowance for the deduction of mortgage interest. The tax laws of Canada, Germany, and Japan have no such provisions. However, some other countries, including France, Italy, and the United Kingdom, provide at least partial deductions or credits.[27] Well known as the effect of mortgage interest deduction has been, it is but one of several features of the U.S. tax system that together have combined to skew metropolitan development in favor of the suburbs.

Employers, for example, can provide parking to their employees as a fringe benefit worth up to $170 a month, tax free. Arguably, the tax shelter favors businesses located on suburban sites with acres of parking lots, rather than the central city firms that can offer their workers little or no space in which to park. (The city firms, by the way, gain no offsetting tax advantage from propinquity to mass transit. For employees who opt to commute on buses or subways, the tax-free ceiling on transit passes is only $65 a month.)[28]

The tax-exempt status of development bonds, which (along with federal and state grants for new sewers, water systems, and roads) cuts the cost of installing the necessary infrastructure for new industrial parks and commercial centers, may also increase the ability of developers to lure businesses out of the cities and into virgin locations in the suburbs. For a time during the 1980s, federal tax legislation so liberally accelerated depreciation periods on real estate that investors, eager to write off the large accounting losses on new construction projects, rushed to overbuild. A glut of office parks and other commercial structures arose in many metropolitan areas, particularly on suburban tracts where developers could erect the new buildings quickly.

The most basic difference between the methods of taxation in the United States and in most other rich countries is America's heavy emphasis on income taxes and, at the local level, property taxes. Among the Group of Seven (G-7) nations, only Canada relies as much on the taxation of income, while Japan matches America's use of property taxation.[29] Taxes on the consumption of goods and services are much more prominent sources of revenue in Europe than in the United States. As a share of total revenues, Germany's reliance on these consumption taxes is one-and-a-half times as large as in the United States. In the United Kingdom, it is almost twice as large.[30]

The differing modes of collecting revenues have implications for urban land use. Tax systems that tend to penalize the use of energy (as noted earlier) and the purchase of household durables as well as countless other items taking up space will inevitably constrain a society from adopting the style of life to which American suburbanites are accustomed. Is it surprising that most Dutch people and Danes do not vacate their tight towns and cities where many commuters prefer to ride bicycles, rather than sport utility vehicles, to work? The sales tax on a new car in the Netherlands is approximately nine times higher than in the United States; in Denmark, thirty-seven times higher.[31] Conversely, systems that bear down on earnings and savings instead of expenditures, and that offer extra tax relief to home buyers, encourage the acquisition of roomy dwellings along with all the paraphernalia they can stock. For most families, such dwellings are not found within the typical confines of central cities.

Local governments in the United States collect almost three-quarters of all their local revenues through taxes on property. To put matters in perspective, the percentages in Germany, Japan, France, and Italy range from 19 percent to 43 percent.[32] Local dependence on property taxation can reinforce a low-density pattern of residential and commercial development. Each jurisdiction acquires an incentive to maximize the assessed valuations of its real estate in relation to the expense of providing local services. One way to defend a favorable ratio is to require through zoning restrictions relatively large parcels of land for buildings. Of course, the incentive for large-lot zoning may diminish if higher levels of government share more of their revenues with localities, thereby defraying costs of local service provision and alleviating the burden on local taxpayers. As will be shown, however, fiscal federalism in the United States compels local communities to be more self-reliant than they are in any other G-7 country.

Intergovernmental Relations

In 1994 the federal and state governments supplemented $479 billion in U.S. local revenues with $242 billion in intergovernmental transfers.[33] The local jurisdictions, in other words, were left to raise on their own two-thirds of the resources their budgets required.

Local authorities abroad tend to get much more help. In the United Kingdom, grants from the central government accounted for 56 percent of local budgets by 1994.[34] National treasuries often finance basic functions that are chiefly the responsibility of local governments in the United States. In France, for example, expenditures by local entities from their own revenue sources have represented only 18 percent of all government spending, and *l'état* pays directly for the costliest service: public education.[35]

With each of the myriad municipalities, towns, and counties in the typical U.S. metropolis largely forced to fend for itself, many resort to competitive strategies aimed at controlling the demand for services and bolstering the local economic base. Land-use regulations that maintain low residential densities limit the number of households requiring public services. By raising the per-unit cost of housing, these regulations can also prevent the entry of low- and moderate-income households who typically contribute less in taxes than they cost in services. The exclusionary zoning renders any relocation of inner-city residents to the suburbs all the more difficult.

At the same time, localities often jockey for business investment, each seeking to beat their neighbors' base of taxable commercial property that in the long run is supposed to lighten the tax rate on homeowners. The competition can turn into something like a bidding war, as the parties tender "incentives" to attract the latest superstore, office park, or sports arena. In this contest, the central cities often find themselves at a disadvantage. Straining from the fiscal drain of their large, low-income enclaves, many can ill-afford the tax abatements, cheap land clearance, and other attractions that suburban counties and townships can offer developers.

In Canada and throughout western Europe, the leeway of suburban governments to play these beggar-thy-city games is said to be constrained not only by the greater fiscal leverage of national governments, but also by their spatial planning powers. The United States stands alone in its lack of a national land-use statute. So, critics argue, development decisions in U.S. metropolitan areas remain uniquely "balkanized"—every suburb is free to "zone out" high-density housing projects, "zone in" commercial enterprises, and in general dispose of its land as it sees fit.

This image is somewhat simplistic. The federal government has adopted momentous policies—the interstate highway system, for example—that determine the disposition of land in the United States, and that local communities often have minimal control over. Furthermore, the major metropolitan conurbations of Europe are often at least as "fragmented" as those in America. The tri-state region of New York contains 780 independent municipalities. But the urban region of Paris—Ile de France—comprises 1,300 municipalities, all of which have some say in the consignment of land for development.[36] To be sure, there are countries in Europe with vigorous national land-use planning policies that constrain the spread of suburbs. The Netherlands is the leading example. Others are found primarily in Scandinavia. In Italy, on the other hand, the nation's statutory protections of historic centers and restraints on haphazard urban growth are so often breached that their administration in some areas has been the subject of scathing exposés.[37] Even the vaunted town planning laws of England have had trouble relieving that country's unremitting crush of traffic congestion and protecting prized accomplishments, such as the London greenbelts.[38] In Germany, the stringency of urban land-use plans varies significantly among the states (or *Länder*).[39] The variability of policy in Germany is characteristic of other federated systems, including, of course, the United States.

Think of the relationship of U.S. state governments to their localities as roughly analogous to that of Europe's unitary regimes to their respective local entities. The governments of some of our states are behemoths, at least as imposing as those of many European countries. (New York state's annual expenditures, for example, approximate Sweden's entire national budget.) If anything, as mere "creatures" of the states, U.S. localities are not only subordinated, but more formally so than are municipalities in Europe.[40] Like European central governments, numerous states in this country have enacted territorial land-use legislation that is meant to curb local abuses. Some states actually have forceful laws on the books, the theory—and occasionally even the practice— being to combat dispersion at the urban fringe.

What is striking, however, is how few of them have noteworthy results to show for their pains. Maybe this is because, as many planners and environmentalists insist, the laws passed by even the most aggressive state legislatures are still feeble in comparison with the stricter rules abroad. It may also be because the master planning efforts of the American states lack the reinforcement of supplemental, if unrelated, policies that elsewhere have helped dissuade local owners of undeveloped land from building on it.

Subsidized Farming

An American traveler flying into either of the two international airports of Paris observes an unfamiliar sight: hundreds of small farms ringing the city. On the way back to New York City, the traveler flies over a different landscape: some potato fields and an occasional boutique vineyard on the East End of Long Island's Suffolk County, more than a hundred miles away from Manhattan, but from there on, nonstop suburban sprawl. Among the many reasons farmland can still be seen on the horizon from the top of the Eiffel Tower, but only megalopolis from the top of the Empire State Building, is that French farmers have been heavily subsidized and, hence, less eager to sell off their land to developers.

American agricultural producers, too, have long been the beneficiaries of government largesse. But European and Japanese agriculture has been far more lavishly protected. The standard measure used to describe these international differences is the so-called average producer subsidy equivalent (PSE), which estimates the monetary transfers to agriculture resulting from a nation's agricultural subsidies and trade barriers.[41] Between 1993 and 1995 the average PSE per hectare of agricultural land in the United States was $67. The average in the European Union was $791 per hectare, while the figure for Japan towered to $12,286— *183 times* the U.S. level!

A major multilateral agreement concluded in 1994 committed all sides to lowering their levels of farm subsidies. In the long run, freer foreign trade in agricultural products seems likely to put large numbers of marginal farmers out of business in countries or regions that are not low-cost producers. The rim of Paris will one day have far fewer hectares under cultivation, and Tokyo will lose its remaining rice paddies. But the changes likely over the long haul are for present purposes beside the point. Through most of the second half of this century, generous support has kept an extraordinarily large proportion of farmers on the land in virtually every western European country and in Japan. Consumers in those countries have paid dearly for this redistribution of income. And the free flow of international trade has been distorted by it. Nevertheless, the costly practice has probably preserved the edges of cities at least as effectively as have many land-use regulations.

Preservation of Small Businesses

In contrast to the "street car" suburbs at the turn of the century and the "bedroom" suburbs of the 1950s, a distinguishing feature of the contemporary suburban scene in the United States is the proliferation of shopping malls, anchored by enormous stores. These superstores are more than a boon to consumers in nearby residential communities; with virtually unlimited free parking, a depth of merchandise selection, and, above all, extremely low prices, the new commercial complexes are regional magnets, attracting shoppers from throughout a metropolitan area. To claim these competitive advantages, the facilities obviously need what densely settled urbanized areas normally cannot provide: vast amounts of inexpensive space. This is why the "big-box" retailers usually locate beyond city borders. Yet, even from a distance the new facilities threaten to dislocate many businesses inside cities. Smaller urban shopkeepers, who commonly pay steeper rents and charge higher prices, cannot easily compete with the huge discount stores and "category killers."

Arguably, from the standpoint of the nation's overall economic welfare, the demise of small shops in central cities ought not be mourned. Like it or not, much of the general consolidation and restructuring of the urban retail sector is unavoidable and efficient. Still, for the cities themselves—indeed for the shape of metropolitan America—the "creative destruction" is no minor matter.

Dense settlements tend to dissipate without a buoyant economy of small enterprises that supply their neighborhoods with desired goods and services at close range. The logic is straightforward. People who dwell in the cities sacrifice, almost perforce, the advantages of greater space, social separation, and safety that the suburbs usually offer. In exchange they expect at a minimum the convenience, familiarity, perhaps even the aesthetic rewards of neighborhood outlets. But commonly unable or unwilling to support the local establishments when their prices soar increasingly out of line relative to the going rate at metropolitan megastores and supermarkets, city dwellers watch these outlets dwindle. Amid this attrition, the urbanites get the worst of both worlds: city neighborhoods with too few services *and* none of suburbia's benefits. Why do so many middle-class families no longer see much point to settling in central locations of Washington, D.C.? As if such fundamental drawbacks as deteriorating schools and unsafe streets were not enough, entire sections of the city lack, among other essentials, genuine grocery stores within easy reach of residents.[42] Hence, like suburbanites, the majority of households residing not only in the capital's poorest wards but also in downtown districts like Dupont Circle, Pennsylvania Avenue, or even large parts of Georgetown, must drive somewhere else to shop.[43] If performing life's simplest everyday functions, like picking up fresh food for supper, means voyaging to distant vendors, why live in town?

Washington's situation is typical of many American cities, but it contrasts vividly with conditions in other capitals, such as London, Paris, Rome, or Tokyo. Here is how an American newspaper correspondent in London described the tight integration of small retailers within his residential neighborhood of Kensington:

> Fulham Road, in our section of Kensington, is what they call a "high street." Almost all the London neighborhoods have a high street, the equivalent of America's old "main streets." By some mysterious law of urban nature, they are always no more than four blocks from your home and most offer more or less anything you need, more or less any time of day or night.
>
> A typical high street boasts a grocery or two, several pubs, an "ironmonger" (a jumble of a hardware store), a few restaurants,

a newsstand with an array of choices, a butcher, a baker, a laun-
derette, an outdoor florist, a pharmacist, a betting parlor. . . .
Fulham has all of these and more. . . .

There's no place to park on a high street, so no point in driving even if you wanted to. That's the key to a high street's intimacy. You walk to the high street . . . , which means unintended
stops, unplanned encounters. It's not long before you're on first-
name terms with shop owners, sales people and lots of other customers. Everybody knows your name.

The survival of high streets in a vast city like London gives a
village feel to many of London's neighborhoods—a small mira-
cle in a metropolis of 7 million.[44]

There is just one flaw in this description: The survival of small
businesses on London's high streets—or, for that matter, in almost
every Parisian *arrondissement,* Tokyo *kinpen,* or Roman *quartiere*—
has to do with more than "some mysterious law of urban nature."
As Jane Jacobs observed forty years ago, American zoning regulations have traditionally segregated residential from commercial
land uses, artificially putting distance between them.[45] European
and Japanese practices appear to be less rigid in this regard, but at
the same time less flexible in another: ruinous competition from
large stores is often severely curtailed.[46] Japan's Large Scale Retail
Store Act, in force since 1974, has done so notoriously. The
French, Germans, and Italians also have restrictive laws governing
local distribution systems—laws that would be deemed unaccept-
ably anticompetitive in the United States.[47] Moreover, onerous
employer mandates hike the labor costs of firms with large payrolls. The volume of family-run businesses in Italy, for instance,
partly reflects the ability of small firms to escape many of that
country's labor regulations, which cripple larger companies.[48]

To be sure, American-style suburban malls are reportedly
making headway in Europe, Japan, and elsewhere throughout the
world. Japan's first megamall opened in Osaka in 1997. Austria
has finally permitted one to be built. Brazil now has five Wal-
Marts. But such inroads are still relatively trivial. For Brazil's five
Wal-Marts, America has 2,744.[49] One new "hypermarket" opens in
France each year, but in 1990 the equivalent of a 34,000-square-

foot mall store opened *every hour* in the United States.[50] And resistance in Europe and Japan remains intense. Ministers responsible for urban planning in all but one German *Land,* for instance, recently passed a resolution refusing permission to construct further outlet malls.[51]

In the long run it is entirely possible that urban small businesses in much of Europe and Japan will go the way of America's, with gargantuan supermarkets supplanting corner grocers, Home Depots displacing the local hardware store, Toys "R" Us taking the place of the children's store on main street, and so on. But protective regulatory regimes have slowed the process and, as a byproduct, have sometimes helped conserve a significant amenity of old neighborhoods. Whether the social benefits of this outcome outweigh the considerable costs is, of course, another story.

Conclusions

These observations hardly exhaust all that could be said about the formative influences of particular policies on the spatial evolution of American cities. One could add, for example, that U.S. welfare policy, with its unusually narrow eligibility standards and focus on single-parent households, swelled the pockets of poverty and social depravity in the central cities, much the way the federal public housing program did. As recently as 1993, cities such as New York were still veritable welfare magnets, with almost one in ten inhabitants on welfare. Well-intentioned efforts to force the racial integration of public schools through court-ordered busing also appeared to contribute to the flight of the white middle class from a number of major cities.[52] Even without this complication, many big-city school systems were permitted to sink to Third-World levels. Families with children to educate have sought refuge in suburban school districts.

Federal and state procurement decisions have often favored suburban facilities. In 1996 federal contractors in the District of Columbia were awarded $4.5 billion in government business. But the suburban counties of Maryland and northern Virginia received

$16.3 billion.[53] Every time the General Services Administration or the U.S. Postal Service replaces a downtown building with one in the outer suburbs, the relocation abets sprawl.

The volume of federal unfunded mandates, requiring state and local governments to pay for everything from environmental protection programs to special accommodations for persons with disabilities, ballooned during the past thirty years.[54] Central cities have often been disadvantaged by these as well. Prosperous suburban counties could absorb the added costs imposed by Washington's requirements, but fiscally weak municipalities have been forced to cover the costs by raising taxes, thereby prompting more of their residents and firms to flee.

How distinctively "American" all these anti-urban policy biases might be is not completely clear. Public assistance in the United States is organized differently than the income-maintenance programs of most European welfare states. Few European ministries of education have allowed their urban elementary and secondary schools to become, as in the United States, a national disgrace. On the other hand, a number of European countries allowed more than a few of their universities to become inferior to many American ones. (However, even some U.S. cities blessed with first-rate institutions—such as Yale University in the heart of New Haven, Connecticut—have remained depressed.) As for such measures as preferential contracts and costly mandates, all governments issue them. Whether the vagaries of their distribution are generally less harmful to cities abroad is an interesting question. Some U.S. cities are required to do inordinate heavy lifting with insufficient compensation—a disturbing trend that will be revisited later.

In sum, it can be concluded with considerable assurance that U.S. policies in many fields—including, but not limited to, transportation, energy, housing, taxation, agriculture, fiscal federalism, and the fate of small businesses—tend to be quite unlike those in other important democracies, and the effect on the structure of U.S. metropolitan areas has been not only pronounced but often unplanned.

CHAPTER FOUR

So What?

The contours of most metropolitan regions in the United States today were formed to a great extent by postwar growth. The same was true in parts of Europe and in Japan, where entire cities were reduced to rubble by the war and had to be rebuilt from the ground up. Nonetheless, the metropolitan population density of the United States is approximately *one-fourth* that of Germany, the European country whose urban areas were carpet bombed.[1] What difference does America's extraordinary degree of dispersion make?

A widespread view among urbanists is that the American mode of low-density development is "inefficient."[2] But if low density is the mode desired by U.S. consumers, and they are willing to pay for it, in what sense, if any, is it inefficient? The answer, according to the critics, is that the social costs of suburbanization are not fully reflected in the prices consumers actually pay for suburban living.

What are these supposed unpaid costs? Opponents of sprawl allege half a dozen types of externalities that suburbanites should, but do not, adequately internalize: (1) the expense of new infrastructural investment and of delivering basic services; (2) the underutilization or abandonment of the existing physical plant of cities; (3) the loss of farmland, wetlands, wooded areas, and other natural resources, such as water; (4) the intensive use of fossil fuels that have adverse environmental impacts; (5) the increase in traffic congestion; (6) and the effects of wide social and economic chasms between cities and suburbs. Given the considerable confusion and misinformation surrounding these propositions, it is essential to unpack each of them with some care.

Infrastructure and Services

"While revitalizing urban centers may be costly, it is still usually less expensive than building new cities—infrastructure and all—at the urban edge."[3] So, the argument goes, if American households leave old city neighborhoods for new suburban subdivisions, it must be because the latter's infrastructure is heavily subsidized, whereas the city's has received little external assistance.

The trouble with this sort of supposition is that the empirical evidence for it is far from conclusive.[4] The undistorted market price of land is normally lower, not higher, on the "edge" than it is downtown. Laying in new capital investment on suburban sites may generally cost less, not more, than replacing (or "revitalizing") the downtown's depreciated buildings, streets, sewers, and other basic installations. Although suburban growth sometimes vaults into empty tracts at some distance from existing communities, thereby requiring separate sewage systems, roads, bridges, and so forth, in time development tends to fill in the gaps, so a great deal of suburban infrastructural extension is actually incremental, contiguous, and comparatively uncomplicated.

The edges of metropolitan areas have received substantial state and federal support for their infrastructures. But so have central business districts when they carry out plans for urban renewal. The final bill for many of these city redevelopment projects has been enormous, often greatly exceeding the costs of comparable capital improvements in the suburbs. In any event, the vast majority of suburban communities around the country now make extensive use of special fees and other exactions aimed at charging developers and users directly for the costs of expanding local facilities.[5] In short, the notion that adding modern infrastructure in the suburbs is inherently costlier than providing it inside older cities, but that suburbia wins out anyway because more of its infrastructure is artificially underpriced, is at least debatable. — long term costs

Similarly, it is not at all certain that the cost of delivering most municipal services runs higher in the sparsely populated suburbs than in the densely populated cities. Indeed, except at extremely low densities, things appear to be the other way around. Per capita costs of general functions, such as operating airports, corrections facilities, waste management, sewers, libraries, parks, schools, and hospitals, go up in places like New York, which have relatively high average densities.[6]

Any direct correlation of costs with density might seem counterintuitive, if not spurious. The state of Maryland, for example, has to spend an extra $100 million a year to bus children to schools in new, spread-out developments, while hundreds of its inner-city schools are being shut.[7] Presumably, the schools accessible by foot in urban neighborhoods and inner-ring suburbs require much less of an expense for transportation. If overall costs per pupil still turn out to be lower in suburban counties, the reason may have less to do with relative degrees of urban density than with the inordinate overhead of big city school bureaucracies and their unionized personnel. Whatever the underlying cause, there is little basis for a conclusion that moving more people into cities rather than scattering them in suburbs would deliver basic services less wastefully.

As for whether suburbanites pay full freight for the services they consume, the answer, of course, is not entirely. The coffers of state governments are funding a rising share of the local budgets for key items, most notably elementary and secondary education. But rural and urban districts, not just suburban ones, are also recipients of state aid. For service provision, even more than infrastructure, there is little systematic evidence that suburban taxpayers are especially pampered (although, as I note below, there may be additional justifications for expecting suburbanites in some areas to increase their contributions).

Abandoned Assets

"We've become conscientious about recycling everything from newspapers to aluminum, but we still haven't learned not to throw away communities. We build them, invest in them, abandon them and start the process over without really noticing that it's happening. As a result, we're mired in sprawl."[8]

However admirable the sentiment behind such pleas for urban husbandry, they beg a fundamental query: are national living standards always enhanced by saving existing communities instead of starting new ones? The dilemma is, in fact, identical to the question of whether recycling is efficient. For some kinds of recycling the costs of the resources expended to perform the activities, including their environmental side effects, decidedly outweigh the discernible benefits. Americans may feel good when they spend time and energy sorting out their aluminum soda cans and carting them off (in gas-guzzling sport utility vehicles or trucks) to be recycled, but the effort allocates resources foolishly.[9]

The same holds for the "built legacy" of some cities. Society as a whole does not invariably gain more from assiduously preserving each existing town center than from simply making a fresh start somewhere else. Does every shabby mining settlement, railroad juncture, or trading post thrown up chaotically in the American West during the nineteenth century merit restoration? Nobody wants a nation of ghost towns, but a political obligation to indiscriminately salvage "communities" at any cost is irrational and untenable.

That said, this country has junked more than just a few western shanty towns or decrepit eastern mill towns; it has also emptied or trashed some more valuable places. No city in the United States is richer in historic assets and irreplaceable architectural landmarks than Washington, D.C. Yet, no other advanced nation has so neglected so much of its capital. A process of suburbanization that only displaces bleak and obsolescent urban relics, increasingly discarded by almost everyone, may be welfare-enhancing. But a process that blights and depopulates major cultural and civic centers arguably imposes a genuine externality. A reasonable argument can be made that the suburbs of America's "orphaned capital" ought to assume a somewhat larger share of the tax burden of maintaining the District of Columbia's facilities and services.[10] Suitably sustaining the historic capital is, at the very least, a goal of metropolitan-wide value, not merely one of interest to District residents.

Loss of Natural Resources

Fast-growing regions like that of the capital have also been devouring land for development at a seemingly torrid pace. Between now and 2020, for instance, the Washington region is projected to lose daily about 28 acres of green space (farmland, barren land, forests, and wetlands).[11] In at least one zone, the northern Piedmont area of Virginia, farming operations are likely to vanish completely. Parts of some western states face worse scarcities. Las Vegas, the fastest growing metropolis in the United States during the 1990s, is expected to reach the limit of its current water supply within the next ten years.[12] A number of new suburbs around Denver will too.

But does such resource depletion necessarily portend, in the final analysis, a net social loss? On one hand, given the scarcity of water, it would seem that cities in the Southwest ought to stop expanding. On the other, a better path of policy might be to allow continued growth but to price and apportion correctly the region's limited supply of water.[13] For in the Southwest, sooner than elsewhere, it is predicted that solar power may enable home-owners to eventually phase out fossil fuel usage.

Preconceptions about the "assault" of urban development on farmland may be even more misplaced. The United States is one of the world's most productive agricultural producers, with ample capacity to spare. Marginal farms in urbanizing areas are not necessarily putting acreage to the use most valued by society. True, some of the worth of these farms is intangible—for example, aesthetic amenity may possibly be undervalued in the marketplace. But if it is, and if Americans really attached corresponding importance to farm preservation, our price supports and protection for agriculture would have to increase. Whatever else European or Japanese agricultural protectionism might accomplish, mimicking it would not lift the U.S. standard of living.

There is a tendency among land-use planners and some environmental advocates to measure the fallout of suburban development simply in terms of the square miles it covers on colored maps. What counts, however, is not just the quantity of land affected but precisely *how* the land is affected. The quality of design matters. For all of the Washington area's rapid growth, the region actually has more trees today than it did a half-century ago.[14] The sterile Levittowns that were once the model for the subdivisions of thirty and forty years ago are less common today. Developers increasingly have learned that clustered developments preserving trees and open vistas are more marketable than barren moonscapes. There are probably at least as many deer, foxes, and raccoons roaming around most of these new sites as there were before they were developed.[15] Granted, some wildlife habitats and wetlands have suffered, perhaps even amid well-planned subdivisions, but the definition of "wetland," for example, is so sweeping that it is sometimes hard to tell how much serious injury to ecosystems has really been done.[16]

The point is not that real estate markets automatically take conservationist concerns fully into account. They often do not. But despite the inevitable conflicts, Americans may still be better off trading away considerable metropolitan open space—particularly if the alternative is realistically understood. Truth be told, the alternative to new subdivisions around, say, Las Vegas is not a metropolis that will be reminiscent of Florence or Siena, but one that will only look like a slightly denser version of what Las Vegas already is. Maybe, with fewer suburbanites watering lawns in the desert, a higher-density "Vegas" would waste less water, but probably not a lot less. As long as the city continues to grow, even if upward instead of sideways, a shortage looms. And if sprawl means the day of reckoning will come sooner rather than later, utility rates and relative prices of suburban properties perforce will begin to reflect that prospect.

Figure 4-1. *Per Capita Energy Consumption in the G-7, 1995*

In millions of Btus

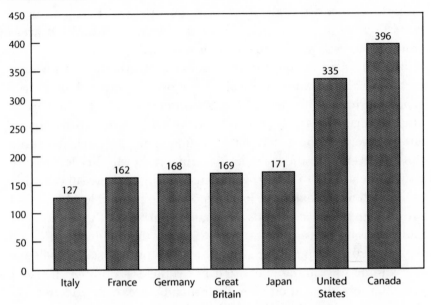

Source: Bureau of the Census, *Statistical Abstract of the United States, 1997,* p. 851.

Air Quality

When it comes to the use of energy among industrial nations, only Canada surpasses America's apparent profligacy (see figure 4-1). The United States does not demand nearly twice as much primary energy per capita as Japan because Americans are twice as rich (they aren't); nor do Americans require twice as much because they typically commute across a continent (they don't). The energy intensity of this country has more to do with plentiful sources, comparatively low prices and excise taxes, and with the form of urban development. In particular, per capita consumption of motor fuel in America's strewn-out cities is four times the average for cities in Europe.[17]

The main reason to worry about burning that much fuel is the extent to which it contributes to the buildup of greenhouse gases

and urban smog. With 4 percent of the world's population, the
United States emits more than 20 percent of the world's carbon
dioxide—more than all of western Europe and Latin America
combined.[18] And, technically, scores of U.S. metropolitan areas
continue to violate federal clean-air standards.

It is hard to escape the conclusion that urban sprawl, which
escalates vehicle miles of travel, is one of the factors that complicate America's ability to reduce carbon emissions into the earth's
atmosphere—and will continue to do so at least until "clean"
automotive technologies replace existing vehicular fleets. For now,
those fleets are on the road and it is uncertain whether less decentralization and more density would necessarily improve other conditions, such as the extent of local exposure to ground-level soot and
ozone. The relevant issue for the quality of urban airsheds is not just
emission rates per mobile source but rather the incidence of pollution exposure. Dependence on automotive transportation—hence
the volume of pollutants emitted per vehicle—is highest in *rural*
areas, but obviously their overall air quality is scarcely affected and
their sparsely distributed inhabitants are seldom impaired. Congested cities, on other hand, often have the worst circumstances.[19]
People there may drive less, but the concentration of population,
and of foul air, exposes more inhabitants to a serious health hazard.
Vehicle miles traveled per capita in Manhattan are few compared to
the levels of practically any New York suburb. Yet Manhattan's air is
often unhealthier because the borough's traffic is unremittingly
thick and seldom free-flowing, and more people live amid the
fumes.[20]

In sum, America's decentralized cities bear responsibility for
some kinds of environmental damage. In time, these negative
spillovers will be curbed by technological advances. Since 1982 carbon monoxide levels from auto emissions have fallen by 40 percent
and nitrous oxide levels by 25 percent, thanks chiefly to better
engines, emission controls, and fuel mixes. The number of smog
alerts in the Los Angeles area, the nation's worst case, has declined
from 121 in the peak year 1977 to seven in 1996.[21] California's South
Coast Air Quality Management District is now predicting that by the
year 2000 the number may fall to zero.[22]

A technological fix for all forms of U.S. air pollution—including the multiple effluents that are altering global temperatures—would have to revolutionize more than automobiles; it would also have to supply cleaner energy for countless point sources.[23] The electrical needs of sprawling houses, malls, and factories, for example, would have to be met by something other than coal-fired power plants. Such a transformation is not imminent, particularly amid the soft fossil-fuel prices projected for the foreseeable future. In the interim, therefore, a case can be made for a policy of stronger price incentives. As will be explained later, current U.S. energy regulations do not send the correct cost signals to American motorists, the majority of whom reside in suburbs. At a minimum, dismantling these perverse U.S. rules, and substituting a higher excise on gasoline, would be a modest but overdue step toward proper pricing of the suburban "car culture."

Traffic Congestion

Propelled by the dispersal of jobs as well as housing to the fringes of U.S. metropolitan areas, vehicle miles traveled since 1950 in this country have increased at almost two and a half times the rate of population growth (see figure 4-2). In the past ten years, the number of miles of roads have increased little. Unavoidably, the two trends have combined to snarl traffic in urbanized areas. According to a recent Federal Highway Administration study of fifty metropolitan regions, almost 70 percent of urban freeways in 1997—as opposed to 55 percent in 1983—were clogged during rush hours.[24] How much national havoc has actually been wrought by this intensification is not wholly apparent.[25] The average one-way commuting time in the United States is estimated to have lengthened by merely 40 seconds between 1986 and 1996, to 22.4 minutes.[26] Because workplaces, not just residences, are decentralizing, suburb-to-suburb commutes now account for 44 percent of all metropolitan traffic.[27] Suburb-to-downtown travel has fallen to 20 percent. The redistribution has worsened congestion at new nodes but has sometimes provided a measure of relief at the older centers.

Figure 4-2. *Annual Percentage Change in U.S. Population Growth and Passenger Car Miles Traveled, 1950–95*[a]

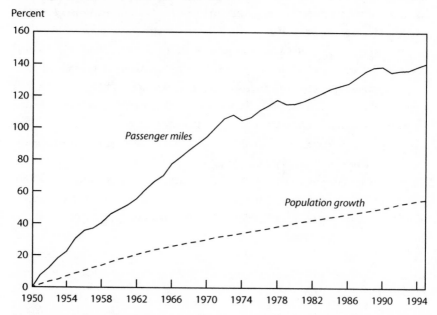

Percent

Sources: Federal Highway Administration, *Highway Statistics Summary to 1995*, pp. V-11 to V-14, table VM-201; Bureau of the Census, *The Statistical Abstract of the U.S., 1997*, p. 8.

a. In 1995, 1.5 trillion passenger miles were recorded for a population of 265,557,000.

With efficient utilization of road capacity, polycentric or dispersed metropolitan spatial structures do not necessarily increase average commuting time; in fact, they may shorten it.[28]

Existing road capacity is anything but efficiently utilized, however, in and around most U.S. cities. Every time an additional motorist pulls onto a freeway already loaded with vehicles, his or her "private" cost of joining the traffic falls shy of society's costs in the form of the driver's incremental contribution to congestion and pollution. Optimal pricing of highway facilities calls for congestion tolls that reflect this *marginal* social cost, which is generally higher than the *average* cost of using and maintaining the facilities.[29] (In the United States, generally meager gasoline taxation captures, at most, only the average cost of highway usage.)

Absent better rationing of roadways through devices such as electronic peakload pricing, there is little question that nonstop suburban growth, because of its near-complete reliance on travel by automobile, will cause congestion to mount in parts of many metropolitan areas. Of course, the old remedy—continually building highways to catch up with the demand—can also alleviate traffic problems, but to resort to more road construction before optimizing the use of existing capacity is to misallocate resources. American living standards are lowered, not raised, by it.

City-Suburb Disparities

In 1970 the city of Detroit had a relatively balanced income distribution. Fifty-eight percent of its families were middle-income, 22 percent had high incomes, and 20 percent were poor.[30] By 1990 the distribution had changed dramatically. Less than 50 percent of the city's families were in the middle-income group, while high-income families had fallen to 10 percent and low-income families had risen to 40 percent. Detroit represents an extreme case, but places such as Cleveland, Buffalo, and New Orleans are among other major cities that experienced a similar change. In some other cities, the income distribution has evolved somewhat differently. In Boston and Washington, for instance, it has become more bifurcated, with proportionally more rich as well as poor, and a substantial decline of the broad middle class. A few major U.S. cities—for example, Jacksonville, San Francisco, and Baltimore—slightly reduced their percentages of low-income families.[31] Nonetheless, the general picture in U.S. metropolitan areas is reasonably plain: on average, almost 20 percent of the residents of central cities fell below the poverty line as of 1990, whereas less than 8.5 percent of the persons living in suburbs were comparably impoverished.

That disproportionate poverty in the inner cores of metropolitan areas can precipitate a kind of urban death spiral is well known. The isolated enclaves of indigent households intensify the social maladies of the inner city. Relatively high levels of unemployment are aggravated by physical separation from emerging job markets in suburbs. And the enclaves breed a subculture of drug abuse, soaring rates of teenage pregnancy, and crime. Viable firms and households in the vicinity of these perils bail out. Disinvestment in the cities deepens as their services (especially schools) degrade and taxes rise to cope with the resulting erosion of the economic base and the fiscal strain intensified by the urban underclass.[32]

How, if at all, does the American suburban growth process render these problems worse than they otherwise might be? In an unregulated market, the cost of space on the margins of metropolitan areas would be almost always lower per square foot than it is closer to downtown. Other things equal, a larger number of low-income households in urban areas would gravitate to sites on these outskirts, instead of remaining confined to the metropolitan hub. Other things are not equal, however. Zoning and building codes ratchet the price of suburban residential space, through large-lot requirements, restrictions on multifamily structures, costly building specifications, and so on.[33] These regulations undoubtedly erect some barriers to the physical mobility of low-income households, limiting more of them to close-in housing.

Apart from the inequality of opportunity the barriers accentuate for the urban poor, rules that immobilize these people are also unfair to some of the urban middle class. Families that are, in effect, forced to depart a distressed and dangerous city in order to educate their children (or even just to get them out of harm's way) are essentially refugees. That these families, unlike the poor, have the means to take flight is only partial consolation. Inasmuch as their relocation to the suburbs is involuntary, some quotient of suburban growth cannot be considered purely a consequence of tastes or a maximization of welfare.

To conclude that the extant spatial distribution of poverty in many American metropolitan areas is problematic, however, is not to assume that swapping it for a different pattern would be unquestionably better. The status quo is suboptimal, but so might be the alternatives.

Suppose government, at the wave of a wand, could have closed all escape routes to the countryside. Consolidating metropolitan businesses and households into central cities would have raised their real estate prices, thereby stuffing low-income residents into costlier housing of lower quality. To offset this economic injustice, housing subsidies would have had to increase to levels customary in European welfare states but probably inconceivable in the United States. A substantial upgrade in housing quality for the inner-city poor over the past half-century has been an unheralded side-benefit of U.S. suburban expansion. As the postwar exodus from crowded cities gathered momentum, the stock that trickled down to the low-income families who were left behind grew less substandard and more affordable. It is hard to imagine how an equivalent improvement could have been possible in U.S. cities if, as in many European and Japanese ones, peripheral urban growth had been more closely circumscribed.

The planning requirements and building regulations of exurban jurisdictions sometimes seem unreasonably restrictive. The codes of some of these outer counties and localities appear so intent on assuring risk-free standards for every dwelling unit, schoolyard, and deer path, that local property valuations effectively price all but the affluent out of the local market. But in no small part such standards also express community preferences. Why should a community's intense desire for safety, amenity, or affluence merit less weight than the wants or wishes of groups outside its jurisdiction? Even the possibility that the preferences can be "discriminatory" does not necessarily make them illegitimate. Think of nations. They too are communities, and the advanced ones tend to embrace relatively high standards of consumer safety, environmental amenity, and labor compensation. These entities restrict immigration on the grounds that, among other things, open borders might imperil those standards. Is this restrictive practice impermissible?

In a perfect world, all citizens would be able to choose their residential communities and determine the character of them with like-minded citizens. In a less than perfect world, some people have these opportunities, but others do not. Stripping the first group of its choices in order to lessen inequity with the second does not necessarily net a gain in national well-being. On the contrary, it may provoke social and political unrest.

"Any city," wrote Plato, "is in fact divided into two, one the city of the poor, the other of the rich. They are at war with one another." Are prospects for peaceful coexistence enhanced by shrinking the linear distance between a city's haves and have-nots? Judging from results in European cities, the answer is not always encouraging. Marseilles, like virtually all French metropolitan areas, contains its inhabitants within growth boundaries that would be considered cramped by U.S. norms. Most of the city's underprivileged North African immigrants populate scattered housing projects, some near the city's edge. The ecology of Marseilles, in short, is unlike that of the typical American metropolis. So are its politics. Since 1984 Jean-Marie Le Pen's xenophobic National Front has averaged up to 28 percent of the vote in local elections.[34]

Conclusions

Outward growth of urbanized areas is hardly unique to the United States, but the sheer scope of the phenomenon obviously is, thanks in part to a particular combination of U.S. public policies. Yet, whether the upshot is on balance unsound for American society is no simple question.

How inefficient is the American suburban growth "model"? Its social and environmental implications are not always fully reflected in the relative prices on which users of metropolitan real estate base their transactions. Some types of putative undervaluation are more evident than others. For example, the hypothesis that suburbanites are systematically underpaying for the provision of infrastructural and service improvements in their communities seems less compelling than the probability that suburbanization malnourishes some historic centers, contributes to global warming (at least given existing technologies), creates some unnecessary traffic bottlenecks (at least absent a suitable road-pricing system), and distorts the selection of locations for some urban households and enterprises (at least given the regulatory practices of some suburban jurisdictions).

There may be additional attributes of America's "spread cities" that are purportedly troublesome. For example, some dissenters insist that much of the suburban way of life is boring, isolating, or vulgar. The dissent is not confined to writers on the political left.[35] Although parts are to be taken seriously, this facet of the debate will not be joined here. What detractors deem boring, isolating, or vulgar is the embodiment of the "American dream" for scores of millions. If the measure of a society's welfare is the satisfaction of its popular aspirations, indictments of America's "rootless" suburbs somehow have to be squared with the fact that more than half of all Americans, exercising their reasonably free will, have decided to live there.

Whatever our sprawling suburbia's multiple shortcomings, proven or hypothetical, weighing them requires a reality test, not an invidious comparison with utopia. Altering the course of America's urban growth by forcing more of it into higher density cities would almost inevitably hike the cost of housing, most egregiously for the poor. Tensions between groups—the middle class and the underclass, natives and immigrants, and so on—might increase, not decrease. And millions of consumers would be dissatisfied. In 1835 Alexis de Tocqueville had noted the impulse of Americans to be "in constant motion," respecting no limits to urban growth. A majority of Americans a hundred and sixty-five years later would still chafe at losing this perceived freedom, real or illusory.

Maybe there is some optimal middle ground between America's boundless suburbanization and the sometimes suffocating urban densities of Japan or Europe, but where that preferred point lies (let alone how to attain it) is anybody's guess. Aesthetes sometimes assume that erring in the direction of Europe or Japan would somehow enable American cities to emulate the showcases abroad. In reality, the face of the American metropolis, however stringently planned for higher densities, would resemble, at best, the rest of the industrial world's banal modernities—not Paris but Brussels, not Venice but Hamburg, not Kyoto but Osaka.

Further, as in many of these places, the heavy hand needed to control development might well exact a stiff price in the form of economic stagnation (see figure 4-3). By the late 1980s unemployment in Hamburg had placed more than 10 percent of the city's population on the dole and left 26,000 people homeless despite a

Figure 4-3. *International Comparison of Employment–Population Ratios, 1960–97*

Employment to population ratio (percent)

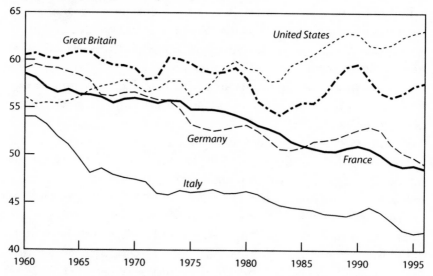

Source: ftp://146.142.4.23/pub/special.requests/ForeignLabor/flslforc.txt, prepared by the U.S. Department of Labor.

doubling of housing subsidies after 1981.[36] In some French cities—Lille, for example—the ravages of unemployment, nearing 15 percent in 1997, have been worse.[37] Even the region of Paris, the most dynamic in France, managed to create only 400,000 jobs from 1975 to 1990.[38] Meanwhile, during a comparable period, the New York region with a population less than twice as large created 1.8 million jobs—four and half times as many.[39]

The tribulations of national economies in western Europe and Japan stem from a lot more than rigid constraints on metropolitan development. It is worth noting, however, that the negative impact of these constraints is no secret to some policymakers overseas. A major report by the Japanese government identified an inflexible system of land-use regulation as a factor "holding back Japan's future development and progress."[40] So stifling is the extreme compression of people and functions in the Tokyo area that government planners see deconcentration as a top economic priority.[41] Likewise, a recent report by McKinsey and Company concluded that lagging productivity of the British economy derives in part from land-use controls that hinder entry and expansion of the most productive firms.[42] Considering these foreign predicaments, the synergy of market forces and official policies that, however haphazardly, even recklessly, has decentralized urban areas in the United States may be less infelicitous than it appears.

CHAPTER FIVE

Shopworn Solutions

Because the hyperextended American metropolis is more than just the product of uncontrollable impulses—and because at least some of the result is cause for legitimate concern—countermeasures have been invoked for decades. In one incarnation or another these chiefly have involved four kinds of initiatives: (1) physical and economic development programs intended to revitalize city centers; (2) federal and state funds to bolster urban mass transit systems; (3) metropolitan growth management schemes; and (4) reorganizations to right interjurisdictional fiscal imbalances.

Notice what this agenda has not endeavored to do. It has seldom seriously challenged the most powerful, and lopsided, federal policies shaping metropolitan development. For example, the highway trust fund has never been disciplined by legislative provisions for fees that adequately reflect the full costs of congestion and pollution. Nor has the agenda summoned the multiple supplementary instruments, such as steep consumption taxes, broad-based rental housing subsidies, and fierce protectionism, that in Europe and Japan have fostered a less outspread style of urban land use. With its limited reach, it is fair to say that U.S. urban policy cannot even faintly "Europeanize" the shape of American cities.

The Rigors of Revitalization

The federal urban renewal program, initiated in 1949, was the first in a series of national attempts to restore U.S. central cities as the dominant metropolitan magnets for people and jobs. But despite billions in subsidies for slum clearance and reconstruction, urban "renewal" during the ensuing fifteen years managed mainly to evict at least a million persons from old city neighborhoods, tear down more homes than it built, uproot more small businesses from re-developed areas than were drawn back in, and *decrease* the flow of tax revenues to city treasuries.[1] The strenuous program did virtually nothing to stem the postwar tide of suburban growth; if anything, the bulldozing of vast downtown tracts scarred some cities irrepara-bly, turning them into less desirable places to live.

With rare exceptions, subsequent variations or refinements of the urban redevelopment campaign, though less perverse, did not fare much better. The more supple Model Cities program of the lat-ter 1960s, for instance, was intended to saturate selected inner-city neighborhoods with a coordinated infusion of grants-in-aid, the aim being to slow suburban sprawl not only by rehabilitating blighted city districts but also by alleviating poverty and social disorders in their midst. Long on targets and lacking follow-through, this federal experiment fell far short of its ambitious goals.[2]

Beginning in the 1970s, federal urban aid was repackaged into programs such as Community Development Block Grants and Urban Development Action Grants that offered municipal govern-ments somewhat greater flexibility in design and execution. Some cities leveraged these and other sources of external support to per-form awesome face-lifts. Baltimore, for example, renovated its entire central waterfront, replete with two sport hippodromes and an oversized convention hall. As of 1990, Boston had poured at least $20 billion into redesigning its harbor, central artery, airport access, various housing sites, and an in-town sports arena.[3]

But, at the end of the day, how much urban regeneration did these immensely expensive projects actually buy? Practically nowhere did the "islands of renewal in seas of decay," to quote

Brian J. L. Berry, stir "a back-to-the-city movement." At best, some may have helped stanch the hemorrhage of population from limited zones of the cities.[4] But this was not enough to reverse the long-standing trend. In 1950 fully 71 percent of the population of metropolitan Baltimore lived inside the central city. By 1990, despite its fancy Harbor Place esplanade, National Aquarium, and Camden Yards baseball park, the city's share of population had fallen to 31 percent.[5]

So-called enterprise zones—localized packages of incentives to lure industrial plants and other substantial employers to inner-city sites—are the latest rendition of federal policy for reviving urban core areas. First introduced in the United States by the Reagan administration, the roots of this idea lay in Britain, where between 1981 and 1986 the national government acquired land, provided tax relief, and undertook infrastructural improvements to attract firms into twenty-three designated target areas.[6] The British experience should have given us pause. Little net employment was generated in the selected investment areas.[7] Nonetheless, the enterprise-zone fad migrated across the Atlantic, where it gathered bipartisan support. It may still be too early to tell whether the costly cocktail of inducements required to draw businesses to urban America's scattered "empowerment" zones will eventually pay off in the form of major *net* investment and job increases. So far there is scant solid evidence that it has.[8]

Why have the persistent revitalization efforts of many American cities met with more disappointment than success in their struggle to overcome the allure of suburbs? The conventional considerations—high-risk premiums for inner-city investment, comparatively low suburban land prices, uncoordinated program funding, disjointed implementation, and so on—have been extensively chronicled. At least three less-recognized difficulties should be added to this list.

One is that plans for urban reclamation too often have been in the habit of competing with suburban facilities on the latter's terms. To understand the problem it is necessary to delve into the details of contemporary urban design. Consider the planning formula advanced by Robert J. Gibbs, an acknowledged expert who writes on such issues as how downtowns can compete with retail malls and strip centers.[9] According to Gibbs, city retail districts need to imitate, not differentiate themselves from, suburban shopping centers. Thus, he argues, outdoor cafes and pedestrian plazas, even sidewalk seating and benches, are counterproductive because they may distract shoppers from shopping. Pavements should be built of no better material than brushed concrete, otherwise potential shoppers might "stare at them as they walk by the storefronts." How about trees? "Generally, fewer will do . . . to avoid obstructing store fronts or signage." A collection of old-fashioned small-town stores won't do either. Downtowns, like suburban malls, need to be anchored by large-scale, national brand-name outlets. Automobile traffic is to be *hmm...* encouraged, not banned, to ensure a sufficient volume of shoppers. Above all, "ample, close-by parking" is essential.

What proponents of such modernized downtowns seldom ask themselves is why billions of tax dollars should go toward helping these remodeled business districts "compete" with virtually identical ones that abound in the suburbs through largely free markets. Indeed, the specifications of the city plans—big facilities, big parking lots—seem tailor-made for attracting suburban day-trippers and busloads of out-of-town conventioneers, not for promoting the intimate urban amenities that might actually entice households to *live* in town. At best, the cities may collect some added revenues from visitors who, for some reason, decide to shop or recreate there instead of the nearest suburban venues. But when all the bills of redevelopment come due, the net return for society or for the cities themselves is frequently nil.

In fact, the cities often resume losing viable residents and tax base. Even the expected boost from well-designed installations rarely seems to make a real difference. Baltimore's much-acclaimed Orioles Park at Camden Yards, like any other modern stadium, is surrounded by a no-man's-land of road ramps and parking lots. Dedicating that much asphalt to a seasonal sport facility in a prime central location may be convenient for the region's baseball fans, but it has not paved the way for an authentic renaissance of the city of Baltimore.[10] As if this conundrum could be solved by adding more of the same, the city has since built a *second* stadium complex, next to the first, this one to accommodate a pro football franchise. Throughout the United States, where governments have subsidized all or most of new football or baseball stadiums, the facilities have proven a net financial drain, with development costs long exceeding incremental tax receipts.[11]

The provision of "ample, close-by parking" ranks high on the list of redevelopment priorities in cities all over the United States, regardless of whether they have good public transportation systems. Washington, D.C., is the only U.S. city that can boast an up-to-date, world-class transit system. But when the D.C. government conducted an extensive inquiry into how best to nurture downtown retail establishments, the main recommendation on which the expert witnesses seemed to agree was that the city ought to relax its parking restrictions and erect more above-ground parking areas (since the existing below-ground garages are "dark and shoppers will not use them").[12] No one at the hearings questioned whether a national capital of parking garages would claim any particular visual distinction or grace.

The race to suburbanize, so to say, city centers runs well beyond an obsession with parking spaces. Boosters of economic development in the cities urge them to engage in, and win, an interjurisdictional contest for industrial base. Harvard's Michael E. Porter, for example, is dismissive of programs that support mere "small sub-scale businesses designed to serve the local community."[13] He thinks inner-city zones should, and can, build "export" industries.

The thesis seems far-fetched. Between 1990 and 1993 (the latest years for which figures are available), 97 percent of the businesses created in seventy-seven metropolitan areas were located outside of central cities.[14] The extreme tilt to the suburbs was not for want of urban economic development programs. Many cities tried to match the suburban "welcome mats" laid out for businesses, but they could scarcely keep up. From time to time, even the fiscally dilapidated District of Columbia would try to outbid the resourceful commercial development agencies of Virginia and Maryland. An occasional District firm would come away with hundreds of thousands of dollars in deferred taxes.[15] Despite such tax holidays, however, the city's business climate did not seem to improve. From 1995 to 1996 a loss of 17,300 jobs was recorded, whereas northern Virginia acquired 23,900 new jobs.[16]

Some municipalities have experienced far greater frustration. A $45 million make-over of "Old Oakland," envisioning two blocks of upscale offices and retail tenants, wound up in bankruptcy.[17] Others have had better luck. Boston's Quincy Market has turned a profit—although by supplying goods like chocolate chip cookies, not global exports. "Whether," as William Kowinski has wondered, "the city can be saved, economically or aesthetically, by the chocolate chip cookie is a question for the future."[18]

All of which brings up a second general point. When U.S. policymakers speak of city "business retention strategies" they seldom mean by that the systems of price fixing, entry barriers, and strict operating licenses that protect countless microbusinesses in European and Japanese cities. There the ability of big suburban competitors to undercut these establishments is sharply restricted by, for example, sanctions against discounting.[19] In the United States the Robinson-Patman Act nominally enjoins price discrimination, but in practice this particular law is rarely enforced. Economic predation is easier for America's retail giants because, in addition, they are allowed to remain open as much as twenty-four hours a day, seven days a week, thereby exploiting economies of scale. Compare this laissez-faire norm to German protocols that force all large shops to close no later than 8:00 p.m. on weekdays and at 4:00 p.m. on Saturdays. (Only small stores are allowed to open their doors on Sundays.) Japan's official hours are similar, although even more discriminatory against large stores.[20] In fact, Japanese law puts so many bureaucratic hurdles in the path of retailers who apply for more than 500 square meters of floor space that an astonishing volume of small and inefficient shops manage to stay in business. Japan sustains roughly 75 percent more stores per capita than America.[21]

U.S. politicians across the spectrum have repeatedly endorsed the abstract principle of seeding more entrepreneurial activity in America's inner cities. In 1997 then-House Speaker Newt Gingrich urged "a goal of tripling the number of minority-owned small businesses."[22] How to turn this sanguine lip service into significant results has remained unsettled, given the unrelenting squeeze from big regional competitors. Countries that have conserved an extensive small-business presence in their cities frequently resort to methods reminiscent of the guilds that dictated market practices in the Middle Ages. Whether an attrition of small shops and firms in U.S. cities can be halted without either countenancing some similar antediluvian practices or freeing these firms far more thoroughly from America's own weird assortment of legalistic prohibitions is a dilemma that many wishful thinkers seem unwilling to confront.

There is at least one remaining bit of bad news for the optimists. For many American urban communities, no amount of business boosterism and rebuilding appears likely to be a match for the centrifugal force of other federal and state policies that, however contradictory, are permanently entrenched. "Back-to-the-city" real estate projects, for example, that try to redeem urban rental housing will continue to run against the grain of government mortgage guarantees and income tax deductions. Attempts to resuscitate city commercial centers will continue to embrace, quixotically, the suburban drive-in paradigm, given the nation's seemingly immutable policies on automotive transportation.

The Travails of Mass Transit

While urban advocates adorn the downtown with "ample, close-by parking," they also rhapsodize about improving urban public transportation. Putting aside for the moment the inconsistency in these pursuits, the belief that vital, compact cities and robust mass transit systems complement one another is not fatuous. If the share of total work trips taken on public transportation were to fall much below 30 percent in cities like Rome, Paris, or New York, the traffic jams and pollution, already severe in such places, would choke them beyond recognition. For better or worse, it is not unreasonable to infer that the provision of public transport is a necessary condition for the survival of old cities as we know them.

Figure 5-1. *International Comparison of Public Transport Trips per Inhabitant per Year, Selected Cities, 1992*

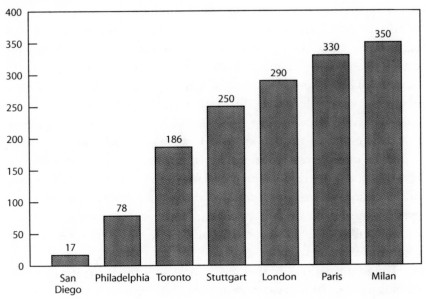

Number of trips

Source: John Pucher and Christian Lefevre, *The Urban Transport Crisis in Europe and North America* (Macmillan, 1996), p. 18.

This is a necessary condition, but by no means a sufficient one. Despite the hundreds of billions of dollars expended to construct and operate transit services for U.S. metropolitan areas, public transportation in this country is a failure. The average share of total trips taken on public transport in U.S. urban areas is about one-fifth the percentage of cities in the United Kingdom and one-seventh the percentage in Italian or Swiss cities.[23] Per capita frequencies of trips on public transportation in selected U.S. and foreign cities are displayed in figure 5-1. In the United States, metropolitan Washington is the one urban area that has developed a comprehensive, modern transit network, but just 13.7 percent of Washington's commuters use it—a paltry number compared with the figures for cities like Genoa (48 percent) or Zurich (54 percent). Not surprisingly, urban transit expansions over the past thirty years have had almost no effect on smog levels. At most, the many U.S. transit projects have lowered carbon monoxide, for instance, by an estimated 0.6 percent.[24]

If expanding mass transit accomplishes next to nothing for most contemporary American cities, some of the trouble has to do with an absence of auxiliary policies that make transit a comparatively viable alternative in many European cities.[25] In particular, no amount of investment seems capable of attracting passengers if transit projects are pitched against energy policies that minimize the cost of driving and land-use policies that produce low urban densities. It is easy to forget that even Los Angeles originally grew up around a massive rail-based system of public transportation (streetcars). Indeed, the region once had more rail transit than any other in the country. The system fell into disuse and was eventually paved over because none of the "European" preconditions—such as prohibitive costs of auto ownership and fuel, and dense residential concentrations—prevailed for long.[26]

Today, it is estimated that more than one-third of Los Angeles is consumed by highways, parking lots, and interchanges. In the downtown section this proportion rises to two-thirds.[27] The area has long since become a synonym for sprawl. What might have modified, or at least decelerated, the spatial conversion of cities like Los Angeles is not just a renewed commitment to more miles of subway and bus lines with inferior load-factors, but a dose of taxes and regulations that most Americans would find extortionary.[28]

Growth Management

Many local governments and a number of states have been adopting growth-managing strategies in an effort to halt the expanding hodgepodge of suburban subdivisions.[29] Although most of these exertions have not come close to fulfilling expectations, some are making an impression. The best known experiment is Oregon's urban growth boundary, which, in principle, denies developers the right to build almost any new structures along a 200-mile-long greenbelt around Portland. On the East Coast, Vermont, Maine,

Rhode Island, New Jersey, Georgia, and Florida have had ostensibly significant laws on the books. Several counties in Maryland have stood out for their exceptionally aggressive attempts to keep local farmland unspoiled and to build a firewall against the spread of housing tracts.[30]

The story from Oregon is not without complications. On one hand, the conservation plan is not phony. A state that had been losing 30,000 acres of agricultural land a year is now losing only 2,000 a year.[31] By contrast, Colorado, another rapidly urbanizing state, has continued to swallow 50,000 acres a year. Average residential lots in the Portland metropolitan area have been downsized, as intended, from about 13,000 square feet in 1979 to 7,400 square feet today.[32] In 1995 attached homes (rowhouses and townhouses) accounted for 12 percent of the units in the city—up from 3 percent a decade earlier.[33] Downtown Portland has boomed. Some $13 billion in industrial investment, principally by high-tech companies, has found its way inside Portland's "Great Wall."[34]

On the other hand, by concentrating growth, the planners inevitably have driven up the price of real estate. The high cost of land is beginning to curtail new manufacturing plants, or extensions of existing ones. Companies such as Intel and Nike that moved in when prices were still soft might soon be having second thoughts. Median home prices in Oregon and Washington, the two western states practicing the stiffest urban growth restrictions, are now the third highest among ten regions of the country. In 1991 Portland was the nation's fifty-fifth most affordable city.[35] Today, it ranks as one of the most expensive, barely better than San Francisco. Low-income households are being squeezed. Property values in Albina, Portland's poorest neighborhood, have doubled in the 1990s.[36] A trend toward sharply higher land and housing prices has been discerned in other communities that imposed growth limitations. Studies of Petaluma and Davis, among other California jurisdictions with moratoria on building permits, found significantly steeper home prices.[37]

Beside the immediate hardships that the rising costs of housing create for low- and moderate-income families, growth controls may gradually sow the seeds of their own destruction, for the development rights confiscated from property owners become ever more valuable, intensifying the pressure for variances and waivers, and raising the cost of preventing them. About 40,000 acres in Maryland's Montgomery County, whose population is projected to swell to 1 million by 2020, have been "saved" (for now) by an innovative compensation program for local farmers.[38] But despite paying farmers to continue raising crops and animals, reportedly 80 percent of these landowners still regard their farm income as inadequate. No doubt they will up the ante. Barring an injection of subsidies on the grand scale of, say, the European Union's Common Agricultural Policy, it seems only a matter of time before the temptation to release more crop land for construction will be irresistible.

For the sake of argument, let us assume that managed growth were to succeed in holding the line against sprawl. A likely implication of such success would be to prevent, as in many European cities, many households of modest means from owning their own homes. In Europe, policies that keep new development tightly confined to the edges of existing settlements give landowners monopolistic positions in the market and limit homeownership chiefly to the affluent.[39] How unjust it would be to shove more U.S. consumers into the rental housing submarket depends on the generosity of local and national rental assistance. That such subsidies in this country would ever approximate the levels of many countries in Europe seems highly improbable.

Another likely implication is that the growth controls would have a negligible impact on urban smog. Improved technologies, far more than new land use formats, will decide emission reductions.[40] In most U.S. metropolitan areas, the die has already been cast; the sea of sprawl is a fait accompli and cannot be rolled back by belated restrictions. In Anthony Downs's words: "All strategies that raise residential densities suffer from one major drawback: they might influence future settlement patterns, but they would leave existing settlements largely unchanged."[41]

Finally, what would the new growth-managed subdivisions look like? According to a representative definition, their "optimal" density and form is four to seven single-family homes per acre.[42] It is difficult to imagine how, from the standpoint of aesthetics, a metropolis filled with suburban houses on 0.14-acre parcels would be preferable to communities that allow dwellings on much larger lots where more trees and vegetation can at least veil the frequent architectural eyesores. Of course, speculating about the visual downside of growth management, or about the possibility of its other distasteful surprises, does not mean that it is an idea whose time should never come. Maybe plans like Portland's one day will be more widely replicated, and their integrity less perishable than some current doubters' conjecture.[43]

Metropolitan Reorganization

Beyond growth management, for which the sample of truly strong regional programs in the United States remains quite limited, is another kind of reform intended to reshape metropolitan development: efforts to overcome local fiscal inequities by redrawing jurisdictional lines. The rationale here is that excessive fragmentation immiserates central cities. Unable to tap the wealthier taxpayers living in independent suburbs, the cities are often forced to raise their tax rates or cut services (or both at once), thereby pushing out more revenue-producing enterprises and households. Presumably, one way to arrest the fiscal erosion and demographic decline of the metropolitan interior is to join cities and suburbs under a unified authority.

Contrary to a common misapprehension, more than a few U.S. metropolitan areas have undertaken institutional revisions along these lines. This includes not only relatively well-known metropolitan-wide operations, such as those of Indianapolis, Miami, Jacksonville, Portland, Nashville, and Minneapolis–St. Paul. By annexing new suburbs, America's central cities have more than doubled the territory they covered in 1950.[44] The notion that only Europe and Canada provide familiar examples of regional authorities governing cities along with their environs is incorrect.

A glance at the U.S. cases suggests, not surprisingly, that annexation lessens fiscal distress. Cities that gain access to a wider revenue base appear to maintain healthier bond ratings and avoid a downward spiral in the provision of at least the most basic municipal services.[45] Less clear is whether the metropolitan "unigovs" necessarily improve society's welfare in other ways. Disparities in services among jurisdictions commonly reflect not only differential tax bases but varying local tastes for public goods. Inasmuch as unitary governmental institutions help equalize the quality of services within metropolitan areas by effectively sharing revenues on an area-wide basis, these arrangements may level local inequalities, thus promising a distributional adjustment, if not an efficiency gain.[46] But inasmuch as equalization reduces the ability of communities and neighborhoods to choose their own preferred baskets of services, the process interferes with the exercise of consumer sovereignty.[47] The logic of such interference is questionable: If public goods should be everywhere the same at the metropolitan level, why not at the state level? And if equal among states, why not nations?[48]

It is also unsettled whether the typical jurisdictional enlargements, such as city-county mergers or city-suburb annexations, do much to check sprawl. Fifty years ago, Phoenix's city fathers thought they had a plan for orderly growth: they would annex neighboring suburbs before they could even take shape. The result? A half-century of liberal annexations made it easier, not harder, to finance outlying infrastructures and thus for the city to spread itself tenfold.[49] The city of Houston covered 160 square miles in 1950; by 1980, exercising broad power to annex its environs, Houston incorporated 556 square miles. In the same thirty-year period, Jacksonville mushroomed from 30 square miles to 841 square miles. Whatever the advantages of such elastic municipal borders, a "city" that now approximates two-thirds the land mass of Rhode Island cannot be said to have condensed growth.

If consolidated metropolitan governments in the United States do not densify development any better than fragmented ones, perhaps a combination of other policy levers is required to produce a different outcome. Less homeownership, exorbitant farm subsidies, more buses, fewer freeways, a three-dollar-per-gallon gasoline tax, and so on—in other words, the full assortment of public circumstances found in France, not Texas, is what might have shifted Houston's pattern of expansion.

CHAPTER SIX

Eight Suggestions

To the extent that the manner of America's metropolitan growth, with its omnivorous claim on terrain and resources, warrants a reassessment, some of it can still be informed by lessons from abroad. However, before considering what might be worth learning from foreign experience, good and bad, I wish to make two premises explicit.

(i) My purpose is not to fine-tune the main motifs of the customary U.S. urban programs, which have mainly contemplated core-area reconstruction projects and enterprise zones, mass transit investments, "smart" growth controls, and various metropolitan organizational rearrangements. Each of these remedies has had at least some trial period in this country, several of long duration. With rare exceptions, they have scarcely stalled, much less reversed, the momentum of urban sprawl. Market forces have generally tugged in another direction, and the schemes have not rested on additional, more basic platforms of public policy. The relative merits of these fundamentals, some of them common in European countries, need to be examined. But most European policies don't allow for free market.

In doing so, moreover, possibilities that are conventionally regarded as infeasible in the context of U.S. politics will not necessarily be excluded. For one thing, there is no point in wondering how, if at all, the experiences of other countries might instruct our policy dialogues if only those that conform to "the American way" are registered. What, if anything, the foreigners have to teach may be of interest precisely because it *differs* from the American way. Further, the menu of policy options should no longer be delimited by what "everyone knows" about political feasibility in this unpredictable society. Before the 1970 Clean Air Act was enacted, who would have thought that our political process would have had the wherewithal to cut emissions of lead into the atmosphere by more than 98 percent within the next few decades? More recently, who would have guessed that a wide-ranging debate about partially privatizing the social security system—the supposed "third rail" of American politics—would suddenly burst onto the agenda? And who would have imagined that the U.S. Supreme Court would have concluded that a civil lawsuit doggedly pressed against a sitting president would cause no disruption? My test, instead, will be primarily whether the alternatives in question are worthwhile *as policies*—that is, whether on balance they are likely to leave the nation better or worse off.

Tax Reform

Ranking high is the matter of tax policy. Were it not for their often excessive rates, European tax structures hold some desirable features that the U.S. system lacks—most notably, a greater emphasis on taxing consumption. Although the overall burden of taxation is lighter in the United States than in all western European countries, the U.S. system bears down on earnings, property, and savings, while interposing preferences for selected economic activities, such as the purchases of homes or the bond issues that help finance things like cavernous convention centers, sports stadiums, theme parks, and strip malls. Further, with the exception of tobacco and a few other objects of pious "sin" taxes, U.S. excises on consumption items, including those that beget serious externalities, tend to be comparatively light. By international standards, U.S. levies on motor vehicles and gasoline, for instance, are de minimis.

As noted earlier, this mix has helped stimulate the drift of population from central cities to suburbs. Here is how the Jones family will reckon with the American tax code: Why should we bother to save very much if our savings are taxed twice—first on our income and then on the interest from that income? Why not pour all of what we do save into as large a house as possible, the mortgage interest of which is deductible?[1] And why should we seriously consider searching for that house anywhere but in suburbia since, among other considerations, that is where the cost per square foot of dwelling space is favorable and where the latest commercial and recreational conveniences are being financed? Life in the suburbs will mean owning several vehicles and driving them more, but this extravagance is so lightly taxed it scarcely matters to us.

A tax policy that influences consumer decisions in this fashion is steering capital into particular sectors by diverting it, perhaps inordinately, from others. If the Joneses—and most other American households—were less tempted to sink the nation's meager personal savings pool into suburban real estate, more could be borrowed for alternative forms of investment, including businesses in the inner cities where loans are often notoriously hard to obtain.

Taxation that primarily takes dead aim at what you "make" instead of what you "take" does little to price correctly the use of scarce natural resources (such as water in some regions) and of unbenign manmade products (such as those that degrade the environment). One rough way to shift more of the tax burden onto what is taken, rather than what is earned, would be to institute some form of national sales tax. (The functional equivalent throughout Europe is the value-added tax.) Another is by raising less revenue from, say, the penalization of payrolls than by levying charges on the things society should discourage.[2] That, presumably, means hitting such targets as pollution-producing fuels and congestion on highways. Here, too, some European governments are farther along than are the writers of American tax law. The Dutch, Danes, and Swedes, for example, have been substituting revenues from higher energy taxes for social security premiums.[3]

Suppose the United States were to adopt a carbon tax. The infusion of revenue would make it possible to reduce the taxation of earnings and the double-taxation of savings. With this relief, the net impact on national rates of investment and productivity growth could prove positive in the long term.[4] Distortionary incentives that influence metropolitan form would also be altered at the margin. For example, some change could be expected in the tendency of homebuyers to keep situating themselves where they can buy "more house" than they otherwise would, or to lengthen their commuting distances, or to be forever favoring automotive travel where alternatives exist.[5] Even if not all aspects of these spatial adjustments were necessarily a blessing, the principal direct and secondary consequence of a carbon tax would be to cut U.S. greenhouse-related emissions. This effect in itself would address forthrightly what may be the single most disquieting spillover from America's hydrocarbon-intensive economy and living pattern: the appreciable contribution to the threat of global climate change.

Transportation Policy

In the spring of 1998, the United States Congress stood poised to spend over the next half-dozen years an additional $216 billion for surface transportation, consisting mostly of highways. Neither the "fiscally responsible" Republican majorities in both houses nor a balanced-budget agreement concluded the year before slowed this authorization. U.S. policymakers had long since cemented some 46,000 miles of interstates, 27,000 miles of urban highways, and 84,700 paved miles of the rural highway system (see figure 6-1). If fulfilled, the latest federal spending spree would almost certainly eviscerate more metropolitan centers and pull another wave of development to their outer reaches, but these objections were scarcely debated. Instead, in the classic fashion of congressional pork barreling, they were answered by authorizing other wasteful outlays—for urban transit systems, for example, that are, and will remain, underutilized.

What accounts for the seemingly incorrigible habit of throwing hundreds of billions of dollars at the nation's traffic problems in lieu of pursuing a more cost-effective priority—namely, suitable price-rationing of the *existing* infrastructure? The explanation involves more than the natural penchant of politicians for pork. The 1998 transportation bill might have been leaner had it not been for the highway trust fund, which by the mid-1990s had accumulated substantial surpluses. Expending this surfeit of dedicated revenues proved irresistible. After several years of austerity (in the discretionary segment of the federal budget), legislators would have been eager to raid any kind of budgetary surplus, even if no separate highway trust existed. But rummaging for road-building dollars amid general revenues would have been harder; without a claim to an exclusive fund, the road-builders would have had to compete with too many other interest groups. Logrolling would have dissipated the available money, probably leaving a lot less than $216 billion for the highway-cum-transit coalition.

The highway trust fund no longer serves a useful purpose. Originally intended to ensure completion of the interstates, it is now primed to sponsor much superfluous road construction.[6] A bulging stream of proceeds from the trust's "user fee" (gas-tax income) is presumed to pay for each new mile of concrete and macadam. The fiscal autonomy of this arrangement skews the terms of public discourse about urban transportation requirements. To the trust fund's formidable defenders, diversion of its receipts for other social needs, including reduction of the national debt, is tantamount to contravening a contract—literally a breach of "trust."

Few other advanced nations have hitched the financing of their transportation systems to a cash cow of this sort. Lloyd George, Great Britain's chancellor of the Exchequer in 1909, briefly "hypothecated" petrol and motorcar taxes to form a "road fund," but subsequent treasury ministers repeatedly poached on it, dismissing as "preposterous" any notion that highway users "are entitled to make binding terms with Parliament as to the application of the taxes levied from them."[7] In France, a separate highway fund was established in 1952: *Le Fonds spécial d'investissement routier.* Although a portion of the *Taxe intérieure sur les produits pétroliers* (TIPP) was to be allocated annually to the fund, the Ministry of Finance soon began diverting the earmarked TIPP francs to other priorities.[8] Apart from the United States, only Japan will evidently

Figure 6-1. The Interstate Highway System and Major U.S. Highways, 1998

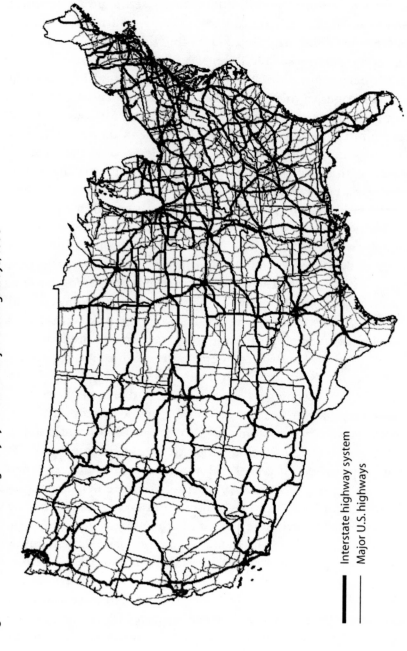

Interstate highway system

Major U.S. highways

Source: Federal Highway Administration.

enter the twenty-first century with a self-financing infrastructural budget like ours.[9] The inflexible institution has been one of the reasons why Japanese fiscal policy remains larded with pointless public works, even in recent years when resources were badly needed to pay down the economy's colossal debts.

NOW might need to re-think when gas taxes up

Nothing the federal government tries—not its housing initiatives, nor its empowerment zones, nor transit subsidies, nor anything else—determines the course of urban land development more strikingly than the national highway program. Its excesses are facilitated by its trust fund. Congress should seriously consider abolishing this anachronism. The 4.3-cent boost in the federal gasoline tax, enacted in 1993, has been dumping an extra $5 billion annually into the fund. If eliminating that fee—which generates unneeded revenue, but which is also too small to induce significant fuel conservation—could help brake the highway-funding juggernaut, so be it.[10] *or put it somewhere else*

Preferable to token surcharges on gasoline would be much more intensive experimentation with high-tech road-pricing programs to decongest the areas most crippled by traffic.[11] Indeed, a rational transportation strategy would set this goal ahead of further construction plans—and would at least delay such plans until the use of extant capacity is made to reach peak efficiency.[12]

Reducing Urban Crime

Few recent developments have been more salutary for America's central cities than the noticeable decline in crime rates (see figure 6-2).[13] But there is simply no way this country can end the headlong retreat of families and firms from some of these cities without an even sharper and sustained reduction in their levels of violence.[14] The carnage in important centers like Washington, D.C., is still horrific: more than three hundred homicides reported in the capital during 1997—more than double the number in London, a city almost fourteen times larger.[15] And the future remains ominous. Demographic changes by the year 2010 could cause juvenile crime to surge again, possibly ravaging the nation's troubled cities to an unprecedented extent.[16]

Figure 6-2. *Percentage Change in Violent Crimes in the Top Ten U.S. Cities, 1990–95*

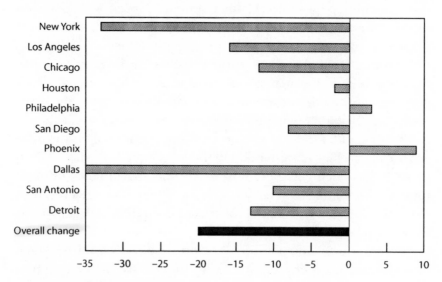

Source: Department of Housing and Urban Development, *The State of the Cities* (Government Printing Office, June 1997), p. 25.

How much can the current collection of anticrime measures be credited with subduing (for the time being) the frequency of assaults, robberies, rapes, and murders? Some of the "get tough" measures—the use of capital punishment by many states, for example—appears to have played virtually no part.[17] Stiff mandatory sentencing has tripled the prison population. Although many hardened criminals undoubtedly have been swept up in the dragnet, mass incarcerations have not been especially cost-effective. California's "three strikes" law has landed in jail one and half times more people for possession (not sale) of narcotics than for all violent offenses combined.[18] (Twice as many defendants have been imprisoned for marijuana possession than for murder, rape, and kidnapping.) Two policy revisions with established track records in various other democracies—namely, intensified community policing, coupled with some restraints on gun sales—seem to have been more helpful than originally anticipated in restoring a semblance of order to a few embattled cities, such as

New York and Chicago.[19] None of the innovations, however, may have made as much difference as has the society's waning appetite for crack cocaine and the simple fact that baby boomers, who were in their prime crime-committing years a few decades ago, are now middle-aged.

For the longer haul, the maintenance of urban public safety will require more than the Brady bill's mostly symbolic appeals for disarmament and a continuing improvement in the management and tactics of municipal police departments, significant as the latter can be. The breeding grounds for young criminals call for action on at least two other fronts.

One, albeit with exceptions, is the purgatory called public housing. Of the past half-century's urban policy blunders, perhaps none left a deeper, and deadlier, mark than the decision to condense a critical mass of impoverished residents into isolated housing complexes. Many (although not all) of these soon became the principal zones of inner-city social degradation and the command posts for superpredators. Washington's postwar crime wave, for example, can be traced in no small part to the relocation of thousands of black families from old neighborhoods surrounding the Capitol into new housing projects further north and east, across the Anacostia River.[20] Policymakers should make it a high priority to close down failed settings like these, as is presently happening most boldly in Chicago, and to convert salvageable ones to mixed-income residences.[21] At this late date, buoying HUD's rental assistance program is of greater urgency than an attempt to erect subsidized, scattered-site replacements, as was done in many European metropolitan areas decades ago. The congressional decision in 1998 to expand rent vouchers—one of the few tickets the urban poor can take to better communities—was a small step in the right direction.[22]

Even more fundamentally, the time is long overdue for a more creative series of incentives aimed at strengthening families, or at least the parental role in raising children. The specifics involve many nuances, and exploring them here would carry me far afield.[23] Suffice it to stress that this society will remain unable to pacify adequately the war zones of its cities unless its parental desertion rate subsides. That, in turn, may depend on less social

forbearance and official sympathy, not only for unwed mother-
hood, but also for divorce and other accepted modes of "self-
actualization," abdication, and absenteeism from the home.[24]
Today, Americans are decidedly unimpressed with the ailing
Japanese economy. But we would do well to remain envious of that
country's low incidence of violent crime—and to grasp the fact that
Japan's unshattered families have a lot to do with it.[25]

Bettering the Schools

While the problem of urban crime is, at least for the moment,
showing signs of improvement, little change can be detected in the
plight of the nation's urban school systems. So long as this impasse
persists, viable, taxpaying households and businesses will continue
to drain out of most central cities and into suburban school districts, where taxpayers receive a somewhat better rate of return on
the fortune this country shovels at public education.[26]

So far, the ongoing crisis of city schools has been met with an
abundance of wishful thinking but precious few reforms that are
proven to work. It might be thought, for example, that adopting
national standards—basic benchmarks that many other countries
use to measure scholastic performance—would be an indispens-
able first step. But in our disputatious multicultural democracy, the
discussion of standard setting has become factional and politicized.
A society that debates whether Ebonics can be a suitable substitute
for English, or whether Shakespeare is worth reading, or whether
instruction in creationism should vie with the teaching of evolution is not a polity that is likely to formulate meaningful standards,
at least on a nationwide basis.

Voucher mechanisms may be promising but are still fraught
with uncertainty. No other industrial nation has resorted to them
on a broad scale, so their widespread adoption in the United States
would be eccentric.[27] In principle, the power of market choice and
competition can be harnessed to upgrade quality—but only if consumers can "shop" with full information.[28] How an informed
process of comparative shopping can take place without compre-

equal opportunity

hensive, standardized measurement of school performance remains an issue. Even with such measurement, how much choice should there be? (Should taxpayers support, through public vouchers, attendance at private schools that, say, teach creationism as science?) And what about the millions of negligent parents who show little or no interest in whether their children learn anything at all? No amount of test scores, ratings, or other data may motivate them to deploy their vouchers discerningly.

These misgivings aside, publicly funded vouchers are "government money." As such, strings inevitably will be attached to them. If past is prologue, these mandates can be debilitating. In time, particularly if federal dollars are involved, participation in voucher programs could carry for private institutions additional unfunded "special-education" requirements, "gender-equity" rules, and countless other commands and controls issued by Washington's social engineers. Programs conditioned this way could wreck as many schools as they improve.

If more needs to be learned about the practicability of educational vouchers, the same is true of the Clinton administration's recommendations. Quite possibly, they will waste money. There is little basis for believing that the administration's three priorities—refurbishing school buildings, hiring 100,000 new teachers, and reducing class sizes—would transform America's sclerotic city school establishments into better teaching organizations. Class sizes have already declined. The national average of pupils per teacher was 22.6 in 1969; by 1995 it was down to 17.3.[29] The reduction did not appear to have made any difference.[30] Per pupil expenditures are already generous in many big city systems.[31] Washington, D.C., for example, spends $7,200 annually per child—$2,600 more than the national average for urban school districts.[32] Yet, only 43 percent of urban fourth-graders are learning to read at even a "basic" level; just 42 percent of eighth-graders are acquiring a "basic" knowledge of math.[33]

So desperate remains the state of public education in many American cities that perhaps any dramatic departure from the status quo may be worth risking. For concerned but disadvantaged families, who cannot easily exit their neighborhoods and whose children are presently forced to matriculate in schools that offer less than even odds of imparting basic literacy, vouchers might at least open a few more local options. The number of such families that would actively seize the opportunity may be nothing like the number who *say* they would in opinion polls, but if the professed support (and comprehension) of voucher plans among the inner-city poor is anywhere near as deep as some surveys suggest, a massive boycott of the worst "blackboard jungles" might be possible—one that might finally deliver the shock needed to rouse city school bureaucracies out of their state of suspended animation.[34] That, in turn, might help the cities rebuild confidence among the remnants of their disaffected middle class.

Small Business Development

Japan has paid too high a price for indulging through subsidies and anticompetitive customs an inefficient profusion of microbusinesses, from minuscule family farms to tiny stores. A number of European countries, too, have impaired their prosperity by clinging to economic controls that, while sustaining a lot of small firms, have stifled entrepreneurs who wish to expand operations and thus employ more workers. As *The Economist* noted in a review of the Italian economy, "Italy's plethora of small firms is as much an indictment of its economy as a triumph: many seem to lack either the will or the capital to keep on growing."[35] The lack of will is not surprising; moving from small to midsize or large means taking on employees that are virtually impossible to lay off when times turn bad, and it means encumbering a company with heavy taxes to comply with mandated benefits.[36] It would be not only impractical but unwise for Americans to ape the rigid employer mandates, budget-busting agricultural subsidies, and medieval retailing restrictions that European and Japanese reformers are finally trying to shed.

Nevertheless, this country's urban preservationists need to understand that without a richer fabric of neighborhood enterprises (other than fast-food outlets, gas station minimarts, and take-out coffee bars), city living in the United States is unlikely to be alluring. Whether America would necessarily be a better place if its core cities had more residents and its suburbs less is debatable, but it cannot be easily argued that most U.S. cities ought to be rescued, at great public expense, if vast swaths will still be desolate environments, woefully lacking the distinctive attributes of urban commercial convenience, diversity, quality, amenity, and intimacy.

How might our urban places recapture a bit more of the character of the neighborhoods adjoining, say, the "high streets" of London? To begin with, conventional zoning principles need to be rethought. Municipal governments ought to cease centralizing commercial activity in downtowns and separating business from residential districts.[37] With appropriate architectural review and traffic ordinances, *mixed* land uses can make urban life more interesting. Second, American city planners ought to quit envisioning downtowns as potential amusement parks for suburban tourists. The only rationale for enticing developers to situate, for example, new suburban-scale stadiums and megamalls inside city limits is fiscal, not communitarian, and even the fiscal justification has frequently proven elusive. Finally, if policymakers are serious about injecting entrepreneurial energy back into lifeless city streets, additional regulatory barriers will have to be dismantled.

By most international standards, entrepreneurs in the United States are relatively unfettered. Nowhere is it easier to borrow money, start a company, undercut competitors, or flee them by moving to greener pastures. But in some other respects, doing business in this country involves unique legal perils.[38] Where, for example, are employers as likely to be docked for "bias" in the workplace?[39] (No other country comes close to extending so broadly and punitively sanctions against alleged racism, sexism, "ageism," or insensitivity toward persons with disabilities. Even unintentional imbalances—so-called "disparate impacts"—in the ethnic composition of payrolls are actionable under U.S. civil rights doctrines.)[40] In how many mature democracies is the owner of the neighborhood pub an outlaw if a twenty-year-old customer accompanied by a father or grandfather is unwittingly served a glass of wine or, as in California, if *anyone* regardless of age enjoys a cigarette on the premises? And where else is civil litigation so rampant and indiscriminate that a restaurant may face millions in punitive damages if, say, its patrons spill hot coffee on themselves?[41]

To be sure, running a business in Italy or France involves larger reams of red tape—what the French call *la paparasserie*. But while U.S. edicts are for the most part less bureaucratic, they are puritanically enforced. Ask brave souls like Brian Choi, a Korean merchant who works long days and nights supplying groceries to his African-American customers in Atlanta's tough West End, and who still carries a bullet in his chest from a robbery of his store in 1992. Not long ago the U.S. Department of Labor busted him. His crime? He had hired a couple of neighborhood kids at less than minimum wage.[42]

Although our city governments frequently bemoan the regulatory burdens imposed on local businesses by federal bureaucrats or state legislatures, burdensome requirements often emanate from city hall as well. Many U.S. cities remain unable to rid themselves of rent control, for example, even though the irrefutable evidence from the cities that have finally done so (Cambridge, Massachusetts, for instance) is that decontrol ushers in a surge of housing investment.[43] San Francisco recently decided to complicate matters for firms with which it does business by mandating that they offer benefits to domestic partners of employees.[44] In 1997 city contractors in New Haven were required to pay workers at least $7.43 an hour—$2.68 more than the federal minimum wage at the time. Washington, D.C.'s municipal administration has compelled all local companies to meet minimum wage and workers' compensation standards, which are hopelessly out of line with those prevailing in neighboring jurisdictions. The same municipal officials wonder why their cities have a noncompetitive business climate and why so many neighborhoods lack the desired commercial establishments.

If there is an overarching conclusion that can be reached about U.S. legal and regulatory liabilities it is that they usually wallop small firms harder than large ones.[45] The latter, after all, can marshal legions of lawyers, accountants, insurance agents, diversity consultants, sensitivity trainers, and all the other management mavens that counsel companies on how to cope with the government's dictates and with incessant private litigation. For the family-owned bakery at the street corner, on the other hand, a single fastidious safety inspection, or the threat of landing in court to accommodate a querulous employee, can mean bankruptcy. The competitive edge of big operators, in other words, is not just a consequence of spontaneous scale economies; it also reflects the superior capacity of larger businesses to absorb the mounting costs of laws and lawsuits. In most of urban America, rolling back those costs would, above all, relieve the beleaguered small fry, enabling more of them to avoid being swallowed by the likes of Wal-Mart or Food Lion.

Fiscal Relief

Merchants and middle-class households will continue to trickle out of many central cities as long as their governments continue to levy harsh taxes to deliver unsatisfactory public services, from ghastly schools to mediocre police departments. There are three ways to bring city tax rates into line with the quality of services they buy. One is to enlarge the municipal tax *base*. Various paths ①
to metropolitan regionalism—including the most common, direct annexation—are, more than anything else, routes to this fiscal enlargement.

② A second device, much exploited in other federated democracies such as Germany and Canada, is for the central or provincial treasuries to share more revenues with municipalities.[46] Neither of these approaches should be dismissed summarily as irrelevant to the United States, although both have been tried here (to a degree) and neither appears to have had any discernible impact on metropolitan form. Revenue sharing in the 1970s, for example, redistributed some federal tax proceeds to local governments, but the formula was so inclusive that fiscally disadvantaged cities were shortchanged. To no one's surprise, many continued to decline.

A third means of easing the fiscal pressure on cities, a remedy that beckons for more serious attention in this country, is for the federal and state governments to abolish or else fully compensate more of the voluminous unfunded directives they impose.[47] With respect to lifting controls that blatantly raise costs for private enterprise, the national governments of Germany, France, or Italy

Figure 6-3. *Comparison of Federal Discretionary Budget Outlays and Off-Budget Cost of Federal Regulatory Mandates, 1977–96*

In billions of 1996 dollars

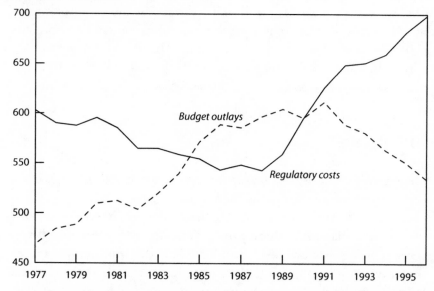

Sources: U.S. Small Business Administration, Office of the Chief Counsel for Advocacy, *The Changing Burden of Regulation, Paperwork, and Tax Compliance on Small Business: A Report to Congress*, Washington, D.C., October 1995; Budget of the United States Government, Historical Tables (GPO, 1996). pp. 191–92; National Income and Products Accounts, Bureau of Economic Analysis; Bureau of Labor Statistics.

are largely laggards compared to the United States. But when it comes to relieving the local *public* sector from uncompensated decrees, U.S. policymakers might do well to study some foreign models.[48] What Edward I. Koch, a former mayor of New York City, once called the "millstone" of unfunded mandates may actually be heavier for municipalities in this country than in quite a few others. The trouble seems to be that U.S. policymakers are trying to have it both ways: Through most of the 1990s they sought less discretionary spending in the federal budget but also no let-up in the nation's activist social agenda (see figure 6-3). At the same time, they wanted the cities to be self-supporting. The result has been an exceptional degree of "shift and shaft" federalism, as local officials often describe it.

Figure 6-4. *International Comparison: Total National Education Spending Devoted to Nonteaching Personnel*

Percentage

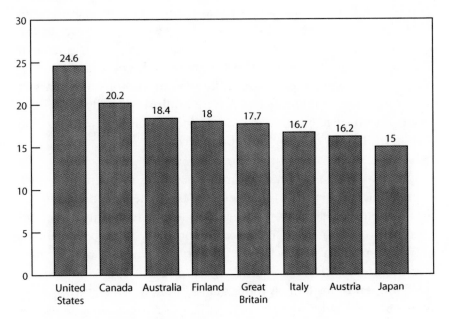

Source: Alexis de Tocqueville Institution, Arlington, Va.

Revisit, for example, the debacle of America's urban public schools. Few, if any, other nations devote so large a share of total school spending to *nonteaching* personnel (see figure 6-4). There may be several excuses for this lopsided administrative overhead, but among the explanations almost certainly is the growth of government mandates and the armies of academic administrators needed to handle the red tape.[49] Illustrative of the problem, according to a 1996 report by the U.S. Advisory Commission on Intergovernmental Relations, are the requirements of the Individuals with Disabilities Education Act.[50] Local authorities are forced to spend some $30 billion to meet the special needs of pupils with disabilities, while the federal government reimburses a paltry 8 percent of the added expense.[51] Compliance costs for urban school districts, where the concentrations of handicapped students are high and the fiscal means to support them low, are staggering. In Washington, D.C., the number of public school pupils enrolled in "special-education" programs increased from 6,290 in 1990 to 7,648 in 1996.[52] Swamped with such students, the city found itself administering special education at a cost of almost $65 million a year, with 14 percent of the program's enrollment costing $21 million. Amid the tens of millions of dollars in administrative expenses are nearly $2 million annually in fees the city is required to pay a cottage industry of lawyers who sue the system on behalf of disgruntled parents.

Urban mass transit in America is another prime example. Its empty seats and sorry finances are no secret. Less openly acknowledged, however, is the fact that Section 504 of the Rehabilitation Act and subsequent legislation have added to our teetering transit systems' major financial obligations. To comply with the Department of Transportation's rules for retrofitting and running public buses and subway facilities, New York City estimated in 1980 that it would need to spend substantially more than $1 billion on capital improvements plus an additional $50 million in recurring annual operating expenses.[53] As the city's mayor blurted incredulously at the time, "It would be cheaper for us to provide every severely disabled person with taxi service than make 255 of our subway stations accessible."[54] Although the Reagan administration later lowered these costs, passage of the Americans with Disabilities Act (ADA) in 1990 portended for New York and other cities with established transit systems a new round of pricey special accommodations.[55]

Twenty-five years ago, U.S. local governments faced some forty federal mandates. The tally since then has surpassed one hundred, and unreimbursed costs have mounted (see figure 6-5).[56] By 1994 Los Angeles estimated that federally mandated programs were costing the city approximately $840 million a year.[57] Erasing that debit from the city's revenue requirements, either by meeting it with federal and state money or by substantial recisions, would be tantamount to reducing city taxes as much as 20 percent.[58] A windfall that large would probably do much more for city slums than would all the planned "empowerment" zones put together.

Figure 6-5. *Federal Mandates on State and Local Governments, 1955–94*

Number of mandates

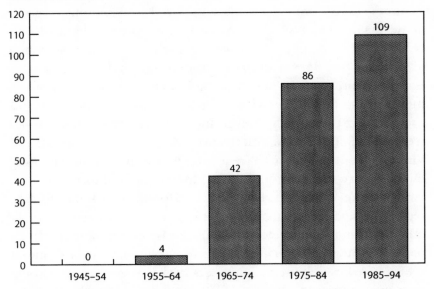

Source: National Conference of State Legislatures as cited in Clyde Wayne Crews Jr., *Ten Thousand Commandments: A Policymaker's Snapshot of the Federal Regulatory State* (Washington, D.C.: Competitive Enterprise Institute, September 1996), p. 17.

Energy Policy

Earlier in this volume, it was noted how policies that regulate the use of fossil fuels can also influence the developmental patterns of cities. The United States has done much to modernize those policies since the late 1970s.[59] No longer do price controls on crude oil and natural gas, for instance, artificially stimulate consumption. But some loose ends remain. Most notably, America continues to be out of step with the rest of the industrialized world with respect to how it conserves energy in automotive transportation. The principal U.S. conservation program, in effect, indirectly assists low-density settlement in metropolitan areas by enabling, indeed encouraging, motorists to drive more than they would if a better policy were in place.

How does this happen? Among advanced nations, the United States is the only one that seeks to save oil through command-and-control regulations on automobile companies. Specifically, these federal regulations—the so-called Corporate Average Fuel Economy (CAFE) mandate—have required auto manufacturers to achieve sales-weighted, fuel-intensity averages for fleets of new vehicles.[60] The main problem with this scheme is that it takes aim at vehicles but does nothing to discourage their frivolous use. Indeed, amid stable or declining fuel prices, mandatory improvements in the fuel efficiency of vehicles reduces the marginal cost of operating them, perversely inducing increases in vehicle miles traveled (VMTs). Today, with the price of gasoline in some cities as low as 80 cents a gallon, there is little doubt that this boomerang effect—more fuel economy, more VMTs—is in full force.[61]

If a national goal is to reduce demand for oil in the transportation sector, the smarter way to advance it is by doing what virtually every other industrial country does: raise the excise tax on motor fuel.[62] By bolstering the sagging market price of petroleum, users of *all* motor vehicles (old as well as new, gas-savers as well as gas-guzzlers) would have an incentive, not only to prefer more fuel-economic cars, but also to throttle back the annual increase of vehicle miles traveled.[63] Apart from conserving energy more efficiently, replacing CAFE with a simple tax would send at the margin a different signal to consumers when they decide among available transportation modes, frequency of trips, or even residential locations. At least a few suburban "soccer moms" might reconsider the imperative of taking two tons of steel with them on *every* errand. The switch would end, if nothing else, the tendency of CAFE regulations to invite more and more driving.

Immigration

No agenda aimed at encouraging beneficial urban development can avoid the question of immigration, most of which presses on metropolitan areas and their cores in particular (see figure 6-6).

The share of foreign-born persons in the United States has doubled since 1970, prompting much soul-searching about the challenges for American cities. It would be naive to assume that

Figure 6-6. *Foreign-Born by Community Type, 1980 and 1990*

Percentage of total population in that community

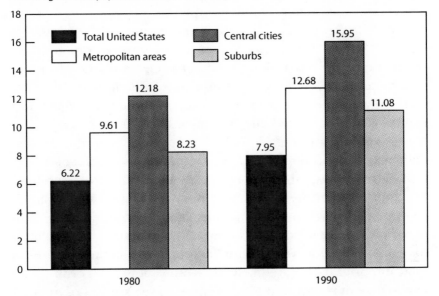

Source: Department of Housing and Urban Development, *The State of the Cities*, p. 42.

the flood of immigrants has come free of charge. It is possible that the wages and employment prospects of low-skilled American workers have been adversely affected—although no one really knows whether the overall impact (to say nothing of the specific effect on the incomes of inner-city residents) has been significant or negligible.[64] The fiscal consequences for communities have also been widely debated.[65] Certain municipal services may incur extra costs. Schools, for instance, may face overcrowding and demands for multilingual instruction. On the other hand, recent immigrants appear to be less, not more, likely to strain services such as correctional facilities. One study estimated that if natives had the same low probability of being incarcerated as all immigrants, the nation's jails and prisons would have one-third fewer inmates.[66] Even if a full accounting were to show no net drag on city fiscs, it is still quite possible that a rising tide of immigrants flowing into the cities and inner ring of suburbs will push more growth toward the metropolitan outskirts. This, after all, has been the historic pattern of U.S. residential succession, and the latest waves of newcomers seem likely to give it new impetus.

On balance, however, liberal immigration looks increasingly like a lifeline for the nation's cities, larger zones of which would otherwise be deserted today. Whether it be New York, Houston, Los Angeles, or Omaha, once-moribund neighborhoods have received a transfusion of fresh blood.[67] Without the 785,000 foreigners that have moved into New York since 1990, the city would have registered another big net loss of population and been well on its way to becoming like so many other towns in this country— a place frequented disproportionately by mendicants, derelicts, and shiftless sojourners. New York has been resuscitated as much by the quality of its new immigrants as by their number. As compared with native-born New Yorkers, the new arrivals are less likely to demand social services, more likely to have jobs, and—perhaps most importantly—more likely to own businesses, according to a city analysis of recent trends.[68] Likewise, large parts of Los Angeles have come back to life, thanks not only to the city's enterprising Asian population but also to the rising number of Latino-owned businesses. (They doubled between 1992 and 1997, to more than 200,000.)[69] While parts of the city remain forbidding, they might be somewhat less so today if the state and municipal authorities had come to the defense of the hundreds of Korean shopkeepers who, in the 1992 riots, suffered largely uncompensated losses of $400 million.[70]

It would appear that America's cities stand to gain more from keeping the gates open to the grassroots regeneration stirred by these entrepreneurial "aliens"—and from delivering to them more of at least one basic service, police protection—than by trying to close the door on them in the name of fairness to underprivileged natives. As a practical matter, the latter is not really a workable option. As Peter Skerry and Stephen J. Rockwell argued persuasively, slamming the borders shut is only likely to create new opportunities for the sophisticated smuggling of immigrants and to play into the hands of organized crime and drug traffickers.[71] Draconian proposals to root out undocumented aliens from labor markets, schools, municipal hospitals, and so on will level at firms and municipalities another barrage of unfunded mandates—arguably the last thing our urban economies need.

When it comes to immigration policy, in short, Americans would probably do well to steer clear of European techniques. What, for example, have vigorous employer sanctions done for France?[72] If anything, a propensity to overpolice the French economy may have aggravated that nation's high rate of unemployment and stoked a rising level of urban violence.[73]

CHAPTER SEVEN

Summing Up

Almost two-thirds of the inhabitants of the two hundred largest metropolitan areas in the United States reside outside their centers. A number of these centers have become mere shells of their former selves. Meanwhile, the ever-expanding suburbs continue to spread people and jobs so sparsely that at its current rate the country is turning over fifty acres *an hour* to exurban development.[1]

The outward trek of households and firms from the old cities is hardly new. City planners have been inveighing against it for most of the twentieth century. And for much of that time, their critique has been confused. Suburbanization has been largely a natural process, accommodating a vibrant, technologically dazzling economy and a growing population in a land with vast territories and resources.

What would American society be like if over the past hundred years the peripheral growth of urban areas had been tightly constricted? Scores of millions would be living in crowded buildings. Housing for the urban poor in particular would be more cramped, more substandard, and much more expensive. The nation's extraordinarily diverse ethnicities might collide more frequently, much as they did when packed into the cities of the nineteenth century. The number of persons exposed to crime, congestion, and environmental hazards such as carcinogenic particulates in the air would be greater than it is today. Restraints on the locus of capital investment would have pinched the national economy, making a majority of Americans less prosperous. Clearly, liberal access to space beyond the boundaries of our central cities has helped the United States thrive and avoid some of the afflictions that especially in recent years have sapped the economies of several European countries and Japan.

But equally clear is the fact that America's urban exodus has gathered pace more rapidly than warranted by market forces alone. A distinctive collection of government policies have spun the urban centrifuge—and observers can legitimately wonder how much of this added stimulus has been in the national interest. Regrettably, the test is not an easy one. Many of the public policies that have shaped development have done so unintentionally. How many U.S. policymakers reckon that, for example, 90-cents-a-gallon gasoline, or a tax code drawing down saving more than consumption, or an off-budget agenda of costly federal mandates can beget major fiscal and spatial consequences for our cities? Intended or not, the central question remains whether the end results reduce the national welfare.

They would if it could be proven that the pattern of urban growth has now become so decentralized as to be inefficient. Individuals and businesses that strew themselves freely across the metropolitan landscape foist a cost on society if they underpay for (1) the infrastructure and services they require, (2) the abandonment of irreplaceable civic and architectural heritage, (3) the depletion of natural resources, (4) the environmental harm, (5) the incremental traffic congestion, or (6) the avoidable and socially undesirable disparities between cities and suburbs. Some of these externalities have been more often alleged than demonstrated. Farmland, for example, is often cited as an asset that is being "lost" in urban regions. A nation does not necessarily add to its well-being, however, by maximizing its farmland. Indeed, it is theoretically possible to imagine a nation improving its living standard by importing every agricultural commodity it needs and having no farms at all.

Nevertheless, the current growth pattern is frequently rapacious, and some of its implications are vexing. The almost complete dependence of the dispersed U.S. metropolitan populations on automotive transportation will continue to tie up traffic and elevate U.S. emissions of greenhouse gases, for instance, at least until the use of roadways is rationed more carefully and cleaner technologies replace existing vehicular fleets. Or consider the fate of historic centers, most conspicuously the national capital. Will the United States enter the twenty-first century resigned to let its mismanaged capital rot, financially and physically, while the burgeoning suburbs go about their business like separate sultanates?

Whatever its merits, the goal of stemming sprawl and reclaiming the cities has remained out of reach of the familiar correctives. A long sequence of programs intended to rejuvenate the downtowns has met, if not defeat, too many Pyrrhic victories. For all their grandiose urban renewal projects, how many cities truly can point to unalloyed triumphs—socioeconomic transformations, fiscal recoveries, or even architectural rewards—from these ambitious renovations? Similarly, generous investments in mass transit systems have often proven futile. Sprawling development continues apace, even where municipal annexation and other forms of regional reorganization have enhanced the geographic jurisdiction of cities. Here and there, serious efforts have been made to bound the growth of the suburban fringe. But apart from the exemplary case of Portland, Oregon, the scale of these undertakings has been modest, and nowhere in this country has their long-term endurance been confirmed.

The uphill climb of these various initiatives in the United States has been steep, absent the primary policies that, as in much of Europe and Japan, serve to concentrate urbanization. Plainly stated, to deter developers from snapping up virgin farm acreage, policymakers have to buy off the farmers. To convert many more solo motorists to mass transit riders, policymakers might have to quadruple the average U.S. excise tax on automotive fuels. To dampen enthusiasm for suburban home buying, policymakers might well have to trim the tax deductibility of mortgage interest and perhaps extend rental subsidies to a larger share of households. The list of such contextual imperatives is long, but the basic point is quite simple: myriad rules and laws influence the density of human settlements, and if "urban programs" can reconfigure those settlements at all, the task becomes immeasurably more complicated where other, unrelated policies pull in opposite directions.

Mere mention of the un-American policy orientations that would have to be entertained to decelerate sprawl provides a measure of the tall order facing this country's urbanists, old or new. Much of what is done abroad is not worth considering here. Even if it were possible, say, to lavish more subsidies on farmers, repeal tax preferences for homeowners, and tie large retailers in anticompetitive knots to protect small urban shopkeepers, such choices would almost certainly leave most Americans worse off.

But not all of America's policy mix compares favorably. Aspects of the U.S. tax system, for example, are questionable. Arguably, tilting taxation at consumption, instead of earnings and savings, could yield long-range benefits for the nation's economy and its urban development. Likewise, a tilt toward managing demand would improve the urban impact of transportation policy, where the reflexive approach to gridlocked traffic has been to supply more highway capacity instead of encouraging consumers to utilize existing capacity efficiently. Urban America's level of violent crime remains unique by international standards, as does the often abysmal quality of its elementary and secondary schools. Without a lot more progress in these two fields, perhaps along the lines suggested in this book, it is difficult to see how the "flight from blight" in metropolitan areas can ever stop.

Nor will it abate if the cities continue to be inhospitable environments for neighborhood businesses. What is suitable here is not to borrow a larger quotient of European or Japanese protectionism, but to make more headway where the United States is said to excel— in unshackling its entrepreneurs. Deregulation, in the form of fewer top-down commandments, could also provide direct relief for municipal governments. An accretion of state and federal mandates will only force cities, already stretched for revenues, to raise their rate of taxation, thereby further expelling the firms and people they desperately need. The proper precept to follow is simply that if the national government or the statehouses deem their mandatory social wish list to be important, they should pay for it. In this respect, the welfare states of Europe are sometimes more honest. Top-heavy and extravagant as they can be, at least some accept a greater share of direct responsibility for the fiscal obligations they create.

Finally, how should the influx of immigrants to metropolitan America be managed? During the 1990s, the United States with its relatively porous borders has performed a macroeconomic hat trick: full employment, robust growth, and nearly no inflation. Our urban centers have received from these conditions a much needed boost. Meanwhile, the economies of various western European countries, perennially preoccupied with sealing their frontiers, have faltered. For all the restrictive immigration policies of these countries, one of every five male youths in many cities is out of work. In searching for better strategies to mind its cities, America has some enviable examples to heed from overseas, but resurgent nativism is not one of them.

Notes

Chapter One

1. Frederic A. Delano and others, *Regional Plan of New York and Its Environs,* vol. 1 (New York: Committee on Regional Plan of New York and Its Environs, 1929), pp. 166, 386.

2. Debate rages on how best to define the pejorative term *sprawl.* In this book I settle for the intuitive, conventional definition adopted by critics such as the National Trust for Historic Preservation: suburban sprawl is "low-density, land-consumptive, automobile-oriented development located on the outskirts of cities." See Constance E. Beaumont, *How Superstore Sprawl Can Harm Communities and What Citizens Can Do About It* (Washington, D.C.: National Trust for Historic Preservation, 1994), p. 1.

3. Clive Forster, *Australian Cities: Continuity and Change* (Oxford University Press, 1995), p. 19.

4. The distance from the farthest southwest suburbs of Sydney to the center of the city is fifty miles. In Melbourne, only 42 percent of the population lives within nine miles of the city center. Patrick Troy, ed., *Australian Cities: Issues, Strategies and Policies for Urban Australia in the 1990s* (Cambridge University Press, 1995), p. 250.

5. William Schneider, "The Suburban Century," *Atlantic Monthly,* July 1992, p. 1.

6. U.S. Department of Housing and Urban Development, *The State of the Cities* (June 1997), p. 16. In the last two decades, four persons moved into the suburbs for every one that moved into a central city.

Chapter Two

1. Bureau of the Census, *Statistical Abstract of the United States, 1997* (1997), pp. 830–31.

2. Readers should bear in mind that definitions of what is "urban" are not uniform across the census practices of countries. United Nations figures, the principal source of comparative data, are based on varying national definitions.

3. Organization for Economic Cooperation and Development, *Strategies for Housing and Social Integration in Cities* (Paris: OECD, 1996), p. 40.

4. See "Open Space under Assault," *New York Times*, November 23, 1997, p. 11. This is estimated on the basis of a 35.1 percent rate of increase in developed land over the period 1982–96 and the tallies of developed land (in 1992) and total state territory; Census Bureau, *1997 Statistical Abstract, 1997*, p. 229.

5. *The World Almanac and Book of Facts, 1998* (World Almanac Books, 1997), p. 541.

6. Data on international demographic trends from U.S. Bureau of the Census, *International Data Base, www.census.gov/cgi-bin/ipc/idbsom.*

7. See Thomas Grose, "Housing vs. Scenery: What Makes England Look Like England May Be at Risk," *U.S. News & World Report*, December 8, 1997, pp. 50–51.

8. Statistics are from Census Bureau, *Statistical Abstract, 1997*, tables 1336 and 1335.

9. Alberto Bonaguidi, "Italy," in Charles B. Nam, William J. Serow, and David F. Sly, eds., *International Handbook on Internal Migration* (Westport, Conn.: Greenwood Press, 1990), p. 252.

10. Daniel T. Lichter and Gordon F. De Jong, "The United States," in Nam and others, *International Handbook*, p. 395.

11. The population of Phoenix stood at 107,000 in 1950; by 1994 it had grown to more than 1 million. Census Bureau, *Statistical Abstract, 1997*, p. 46.

12. On mobility, see Kristin A. Hansen, "Geographical Mobility: March 1995 to March 1996," *Current Population Reports, P20–497*, p. 1.

13. Robert J. Sampson, Stephen W. Raudenbush, and Felton Earls, "Neighborhood and Violent Crime: A Multilevel Study of Collective Efficacy," *Science*, vol. 277 (August 15, 1997), and Felton J. Earls and Christy A. Visher, "Project on Human Development in Chicago Neighborhoods: A Research Update," *National Institute of Justice*, February 1997.

14. Derek Bok, *The State of the Nation: Government and the Quest for a Better Society* (Harvard University Press, 1996), p. 220. American cities differ little from foreign ones of similar size with respect to rates of theft. But violent thefts, or robberies, are more common and deadly in this country.

In 1992 there were seven deaths in London resulting from a robbery or burglary; in New York City, there were 378. James Q. Wilson, "Hostility in America," *New Republic*, August 25, 1997. For a general report on British crime rates, see "The Britain Audit: Crime; Bewitched, Bothered and Bewildered," *The Economist*, August 28, 1993.

15. Department of Justice, *Criminal Victimization 1996: Changes 1995–96 with Trends 1993–96*, NCJ-165812 (1997), p. 5. In 1990 the average violent crime rate in 159 U.S. central cities was almost 1.8 times higher than the U.S. average. Anthony Downs, "Relating Suburban Sprawl to Urban Decline," unpublished manuscript, Brookings, October 1997, p. 57. Incidents of violent crime inside the District of Columbia, for example, were almost *six times* more frequent than in the city's suburbs. Brooke A. Masters and Michael D. Shear, "As Suburbia Surges, Violence Tags Along," *Washington Post*, April 5, 1998, p. 20.

16. Berry Cullen and Steven D. Levitt, *Crime, Urban Flight, and the Consequences for Cities* (Cambridge, Mass.: National Bureau of Economic Research, Working Paper 5737, September 1996). See also Richard Morin, "Unconventional Wisdom: New Facts and Hot Stats from the Social Sciences," *Washington Post*, May 18, 1997, p. C5.

17. Despite a recent decline of violent crime reported in a number of cities, most cities remain deadly and dangerous by international standards. New York's murder rate dropped by two-thirds between 1991 and 1997, yet there were still 767 murders committed in 1997. Meanwhile, in London, which is about the same size, there were less than 130. "America's Cities: They Can Yet Be Resurrected," *The Economist*, January 10, 1998, p. 17. One of America's worst killing fields has been the nation's capital. There, in a thirty-six-hour period in 1997, the *Washington Post* reported no fewer than eight separate murders. So common is such carnage in this city that the *Post* only ran the story *on the third page* of the newspaper's *second section*. Brian Mooar and Avis Thomas-Lester, "Eight Slain in District in 36 Hours of Violence," *Washington Post*, June 5, 1997, p. B3. Lest it be thought that Washington's violent crime is confined to its poorest wards, one month later three people were murdered at a Starbucks cafe in upper Georgetown, one of the city's toniest neighborhoods. During a typical, randomly selected week in November 1997 there were no fewer than eighty reported robberies and thefts in Northwest Washington, many at gun point and involving assaults. Alicia Cypress and Gerri Marmer, "Crime Watch," *Washington Post*, December 11, 1997, p. DC4.

18. Institute for Research in Social Sciences, University of North Carolina (April 1992): *www.irss.unc.edu:80/tempdocs.*

19. The Ninety-First American Assembly, *Community Capitalism: Rediscovering the Markets of America's Urban Neighborhoods* (Columbia University, the American Assembly, 1997), p. 17.

20. For these statistics, and those that follow, see Census Bureau, *Statistical Abstract, 1997,* p. 835.

21. Data from the Council of Europe are reported in "Millions Want to Come," *The Economist,* April 4, 1998, p. 55. U.S. statistics from Barbara Vobejda, "Survey: U.S. Population about 10% Foreign-Born," *Washington Post,* April 10, 1998, p. A11.

22. For an excellent attempt to chronicle the situation, see John Higham, *Strangers in the Land: Patterns of American Nativism, 1860–1925* (New Brunswick, N.J.: Rutgers University Press, 1988). Most of my examples are drawn from this text.

23. The Italians, like the Germans and Irish, eventually found greater safety in numbers. By 1930, for instance, there were more persons of Italian ancestry in New York than in Rome.

24. Stephan Thernstrom and Abigail Thernstrom, *America in Black and White: One Nation, Indivisible* (Simon & Schuster, 1997). By the mid-1990s, 42 percent of African Americans owned their own homes and more than 30 percent of the black population had moved to suburbs.

25. The alternative to this proposition is the so-called contact hypothesis: proximity, or contact, among people of differing ethnicities gradually reduces friction. As a broad generalization, the contact thesis appears to be more tenable with respect to interactions among individuals than *groups.* See H. D. Forbes, *Ethnic Conflict: Commerce, Culture, and the Contact Hypothesis* (Yale University Press, 1997), p. 200.

26. Sam Bass Warner, *Streetcar Suburbs: The Process of Growth in Boston, 1870–1900* (Harvard University Press, 1962). The appeal of suburbia can be traced at least to the eighteenth century when the rising bourgeoisie in cities such as London began aspiring to "villas" in the countryside around the metropolis. Robert Fishman, *Bourgeois Utopias: The Rise and Fall of Suburbia* (Basic Books, 1987), chaps. 1 and 2.

27. Figures are in B. R. Mitchell, *International Historical Statistics: The Americas, 1750–1988,* 2d ed. (New York: Stockton Press, 1993), and B. R. Mitchell, *International Historical Statistics: Europe, 1750–1988,* 3d ed. (New York: Stockton Press, 1992).

28. James J. Flink, *The Automobile Age* (MIT Press, 1988), p. 80.

29. Germany, Europe's industrial powerhouse, had but one car for every 196 inhabitants in 1927. Flink, *The Automobile Age,* pp. 129, 131.

Chapter Three

1. How much of the contemporary spatial structure of polycentric cities can be explained by economic theory is a complex and unresolved

question. Extant spatial economic models, such as von Thünen's ring scheme, at best shed limited light on the phenomenon. For a full discussion of the state of the art, see Paul Krugman, *Development, Geography, and Economic Theory* (MIT Press, 1996), chap. 2.

2. See Robert Geddes, "Metropolis Unbound: The Sprawling American City and the Search for Alternatives," *American Prospect,* November–December, 1997, p. 40.

3. Roger J. Vaughan, Anthony H. Pascal, and Mary E. Vaiana, *The Urban Impacts of Federal Policies: Vol. 1, Overview* (Santa Monica, Calif.: RAND, August 1980), p. 2.

4. *Historical Tables of the 1998 Budget of the United States,* pp. 145–49.

5. American Public Transit Association, *Transit Fact Book, 1997,* p. 62.

6. *Transit Fact Book, 1997,* p. 51. In 1995 public transit in the United States received $8.6 billion in operating subsidies and $5.3 billion in capital assistance. Clifford Winston and Chad Shirley, *Alternate Route: Toward Efficient Urban Transportation* (Brookings, 1998), p. 10.

7. Alan Altshuler, *The Urban Transportation System: Politics and Policy Innovation* (MIT Press, 1979), p. 22, and U.S. Department of Transportation, *National Transportation Statistics, 1995* (1995), p. 64.

8. Pietro S. Nivola and Robert W. Crandall, *The Extra Mile: Rethinking Energy Policy for Automotive Transportation* (Brookings, 1995), p. 62.

9. This was how the British and French transport budgets broke out in 1993. Department of Transport, *Transport Statistics, Great Britain* (London: Government Statistical Service, 1995), p. 29; INSEE, *Les Transports en 1995* (DAEI/SES-INSEE, 1995), p. 164.

10. See, for instance, James J. MacKenzie, Roger C. Dower, and Donald D. T. Chen, *The Going Rate: What It Really Costs to Drive* (Washington, D.C.: World Resources Institute, June 1992), p. 23.

11. This is not to say that each motorist is paying the full marginal cost of using highways. In a subsequent section, the need for marginal cost pricing to increase the efficiency of automotive transport will be discussed.

12. See Dick Armey and Mitch McConnell, "Tackling the High Cost of Driving," *Washington Post,* December 3, 1997, p. A25.

13. Deborah Gordon, *Steering a New Course: Transportation, Energy, and the Environment* (Cambridge, Mass.: Union of Concerned Scientists, 1991), p. 42. James L. MacKenzie, "Toward a Sustainable Energy Future: The Critical Role of Rational Energy Pricing," *WRI Issues and Ideas* (Washington, D.C.: World Resources Institute, May 1991), p. 8.

14. Lee Schipper and others, "Fuel Prices, Automobile Fuel Economy, and Fuel Use for Land Travel" (Berkeley, Calif.: Lawrence Berkeley Laboratory, 1992), p. 9.

15. *UN Energy Statistics Yearbook, 1994* (New York: United Nations, 1996), pp. 167–76.

16. For a comprehensive account see Pietro S. Nivola, *The Politics of Energy Conservation* (Brookings, 1986).

17. Average electric rates circa 1980 were estimated to be one-third below the actual marginal price of electricity for industrial users and almost one-quarter below the marginal price for residential consumers (in 1980 dollars per million Btus). See John H. Gibbons and William U. Chandler, *Energy: The Conservation Revolution* (Plenum Press, 1981), p. 140.

18. The pattern is detailed by Kenneth T. Jackson, *Crabgrass Frontier: The Suburbanization of the United States* (Oxford University Press, 1985), chap. 11, especially pp. 204–09.

19. One of the best descriptions of this perverse process is Arnold R. Hirsch, *Making the Second Ghetto: Race and Housing in Chicago, 1940–1960* (Cambridge University Press, 1983). Hirsch shows how local officials in Chicago, with the acquiescence of the federal authorities, rejected plans to place public housing in "virgin" territory, and insisted instead on situating new projects in the slums. Only now has federal policy begun to undo the damage. The task will be a tall order. Downs notes that in 1990, in eighty-three metropolitan statistical areas for which data were available for both cities and their suburbs, about 10 million persons lived in census tracts in which 40 percent or more of the residents had incomes below the poverty line. About 7.5 million resided in the central cities. Over 19 percent of all central city residents were poor, compared with 8.4 percent of all suburban residents. Anthony Downs, "Relating Suburban Sprawl to Urban Decline," unpublished paper, Brookings Institution, October 1997, pp. 5, 55. Restrictive rules governing eligibility for public housing contributed to this concentration of poverty. By restricting public housing to the very poor, the percentage of working families in these complexes declined by more than one-half since the 1980s. U.S. Department of Housing and Urban Development, *Issue Brief,* May 30, 1996, p. 1.

20. See Anthony Downs, "Contrasting Strategies for the Economic Development of Metropolitan Areas in the United States and Western Europe," in Anita A. Summers, Paul C. Cheshire, and Lanfranco Senn, eds., *Urban Change in the United States and Western Europe: Comparative Analysis and Policy* (Washington, D.C.: Urban Institute, 1993).

21. Margaret Weir, "The Politics of Racial Isolation in Europe and America," in Paul E. Peterson, ed., *Classifying by Race* (Princeton University Press, 1995), pp. 220–21.

22. In recent years, amid chronic unemployment and immigration-related tensions, conditions in quite a few of the housing projects of major French cities reportedly have come to resemble those in some U.S. cities, with rising crime and social disorder. Exactly how comparable the conditions have become is difficult to say, however. Violent crime in France has

not reached U.S. levels. Extreme social degeneracy has besieged many U.S. public housing projects for decades.

23. Weir, "Politics of Racial Isolation," p. 231.

24. Bureau of the Census, *State and Metropolitan Areas Data Book, 1997–98*, 5th ed. (1998), p. 177.

25. Weir, "Politics of Racial Isolation," p. 230. By the end of the 1970s, fully one-third of British households resided in council housing.

26. On progress under the Section 8 program, see Margery Austin Turner, "Affirmatively Furthering Fair Housing: The Performance of Tenant-Based Assistance in Six Metropolitan Areas," unpublished draft, Urban Institute, Washington, D.C., January 15, 1998.

27. Organization for Economic Cooperation and Development, *Taxation in OECD Countries* (Paris: OECD, 1993), p. 36. The ensuing discussion draws on comparative data in this report.

28. E. J. Dionne, "Where Would You Like to Live?" *Washington Post,* July 29, 1997.

29. The G-7 countries are Canada, France, Germany, Italy, Japan, the United Kingdom, and the United States. Actually, the Japanese tax falls heavily on capital gains from the sale of real estate. The effect of this is to discourage land sales for development. In theory, local dependence on real estate taxes in the United States could also suppress development by raising prices. Here, however, a principal consequence has been to lower the *density* of construction, in large part because of the jurisdictional "tax competition" discussed below.

30. Organization for Economic Development and Cooperation, *Revenue Statistics, 1965–1996* (Paris: OECD, 1997), p. 77.

31. John Pucher, "Urban Travel Behavior as the Outcome of Public Policy," *Journal of the American Planning Association,* vol. 54 (Autumn 1988), p. 513.

32. OECD, *Revenue Statistics, 1965–1996,* Part VI.

33. Census Bureau, *Statistical Abstract, 1997,* p. 300.

34. Tim Blackman, *Urban Policy in Practice* (London: Routledge, 1995), p. 71.

35. Edmond Preteceille, "From Centralization to Decentralization: Social Restructuring and French Local Government," in Chris Pickvance and Edmond Preteceille, eds., *State Restructuring and Local Power: A Comparative Perspective* (London: Pinter Publishers, 1991), p. 138.

36. Galia Burgel and Guy Burgel, "Global Trends and City Policies: Friends and Foes of Urban Development?" in Michael A. Cohen and others, eds., *Preparing for the Urban Future: Global Pressures and Local Forces* (Washington, D.C.: Woodrow Wilson Center, 1996), p. 324.

37. Antonio Cederna, *Brandelli d'italia: come distruggere il bel paese* (Roma: Newton Compton, 1991).

38. "Driving Britain off the Roads," *The Economist*, January 24, 1998, pp. 55–56.

39. Despite the existence of national urban development guidelines intended to sustain "central places," a 1993 OECD study of six German cities—Dusseldorf, Freiburg, Heidelberg, Berlin, Lubeck, and Schwerin—found that all reported an increasing proportion of their metropolitan populations living in the suburbs and a declining proportion of metropolitan area jobs located in their central business districts, from 1970 to 1990. See John Pucher and Christian Lefevre, *The Urban Transport Crisis in Europe and North America* (London: Macmillan Press, 1996), p. 49.

40. The legal status of American municipal corporations—indeed, of American local governments in general—contrasts with the European one. The American localities can do *only* what their state legislatures expressly permit. By contrast, European municipalities (many of which hold ancient charters and privileges that predate the nation states themselves) can do anything that is *not* expressly forbidden. It is true that most of the U.S. states have consented to home-rule charters for their municipalities, but in principle the state legislatures can revoke or abridge these concessions at will. For what remains the most readable review of the constitutional position of local authorities in the United States, see Edward C. Banfield and James Q. Wilson, *City Politics* (Harvard University Press, 1963), chap. 5.

41. Organization for Economic Cooperation and Development, *Agricultural Policies in OECD Countries: Measurement of Support and Background Information, 1997* (Paris: OECD, 1997), p. 41.

42. By "genuine grocery stores," I do not mean the equivalent of 7-Eleven convenience stores, CVS Pharmacies, or even ubiquitous Starbucks coffee shops. These chains are everywhere, but they are no substitute for the neighborhood butcher shops, bakeries, or fresh produce and fish markets that have survived only in the boroughs of a few American cities (Manhattan, for instance) but were once relatively common. Between 1990 and 1995 the District of Columbia lost 1,800 firms, twice as many as moved in. Only some of these were the types of neighborhood businesses I have in mind, but the loss is nonetheless indicative of a commercial erosion that detracts from city life. Peter Behr, "D.C. Lost 955 Employers in 5 Years, Analysis Finds," *Washington Post*, January 7, 1997.

43. The problem along Pennsylvania Avenue is illustrative. A valiant effort has been made to transform this boulevard into more than a long parade of faceless government office buildings. At least one elegant residential complex (at the site of the Navy Memorial, opposite the National Archives) was introduced. "But," as a recent account of this project notes, "the city's 16-year-old dream of a 'living downtown' hasn't come true yet, and there is evidence the roots need fortifying. The Lansburgh Market, the neighborhood's little food store, closed over the summer. To buy groceries,

residents have to go to more-populated city neighborhoods or to the suburbs." David Montgomery, "Not Quite a Neighborhood," *Washington Post,* October 23, 1997, p. A1.

44. Fred Barbash, "Farewell to the London High Street, Where Everybody Knew Our Names," *Washington Post,* August 31, 1997, p. C5.

45. Jane Jacobs, *The Death and Life of Great American Cities* (Random House, 1961).

46. For a comparative perspective on U.S. zoning practices, see George W. Liebmann, "Modernization of Zoning: A Means to Reform," *Regulation,* no. 2 (1996).

47. Patrick A. Messerlin, "How to Wreck the WTO," *Wall Street Journal,* July 23, 1997. The protection of small retailers in Italy is in part a vestige of the fascist period. See Vera Negri Zamagni, *La distribuzione commerciale in Italia fra le due guerre* (Milan: F. Agnelli, 1981). Italy has recently moved to liberalize parts of its retail regulations. Even so, to protect small shopkeepers, no additional operating licenses will be granted for new "hypermarkets." "Italy: Open Up!" *The Economist,* March 14, 1998, p. 59.

48. See "Italian Small Businesses: Change in the Heartland," *The Economist,* April 2, 1994, p. 63. Demographic and household composition of many Italian cities also helps explain the staying power of small downtown retailers. Low birth rates, small households, and an aging population create a steady clientele. In cities such as Genoa, Bologna, and Trieste the proportion of residents sixty-five years old or more now ranges from one-fifth to almost one-quarter. Figures provided by the *Settore Pianificazione e Controllo del Commune di Bologna* (1998).

49. Wendy Zellneret and others, "Wal-Mart Spoken Here," *Business Week,* June 23, 1997, p. 139.

50. Michael Reid, "All the World's a Shop," *The Economist,* March 4, 1995, p. SS15; Donella Meadows, "Malling America: How to Stop a Superstore Takeover," *The Amicus Journal,* vol. 16, no. 4 (Winter 1995), p. 12. The number of shopping centers, including malls, in the United States increased nearly 48 percent from 1986 to 1996, from 28,496 to 42,130. Kerry Hannon and William Holstein, "They Drop Till You Shop," *U.S. News & World Report,* July 21, 1997, p. 51.

51. Ernest Beck, "American-Style Outlet Malls in Europe Make Headway Despite Local Resistance," *Wall Street Journal,* September 17, 1997.

52. There was, of course, considerable debate on this point. See, on one hand, Diane Ravitch, "The 'White Flight' Controversy," *The Public Interest,* no. 1 (Spring 1978) and Nathan Glazer, *Affirmative Discrimination: Ethnic Inequality and Public Policy* (Basic Books, 1975), pp. 120–23. But on the other hand, Gary Orfield, *Must We Bus? Segregated Schools and National Policy* (Brookings, 1978), pp. 99–101.

53. Peter Behr, "Contractors Set Record for Orders," *Washington Post,* February 24, 1997, p. A8.

54. See U.S. Advisory Commission on Intergovernmental Relations, *The Role of Federal Mandates in Intergovernmental Relations* (Washington, D.C.: ACIR, January 1996).

Chaper Four

1. Census Bureau, *Statistical Abstract, 1997,* Appendix II, Table A, p. 940; Rainer Mackensen, "Urban Decentralization Processes in Western Europe," in Anita A. Summers, Paul C. Cheshire, and Lanfranco Senn, eds., *Urban Change in the United States and Western Europe: Comparative Analysis and Policy* (Washington, D.C.: Urban Institute, 1993), p. 319.

2. Richard B. Peiser, "Density and Urban Sprawl," *Land Economics,* August 1989, pp. 193–204.

3. "Competition for Land,"*American Farmland,* vol. 17, no. 3 (Fall 1996), p. 15.

4. There is evidence that in rapidly growing urban areas new development is not paying its way. However, whether this result is a function of the *density* of that development is an unsettled question. See Helen F. Ladd, *Effects of Population Growth on Local Spending and Taxes* (Cambridge, Mass.: Lincoln Institute of Land Policy, 1992).

5. See Alan A. Altshuler and José A. Gómez-Ibáñez, *Regulation for Revenue: The Political Economy of Land Use Exactions* (Brookings and Lincoln Institute of Land Policy, 1993).

6. Helen F. Ladd and John Yinger, *America's Ailing Cities: Fiscal Health and the Design of Urban Policy* (Johns Hopkins University Press, 1989), p. 85. In subsequent research, Ladd concluded more forcefully that "the basic message is that beyond the relatively low average density of 250 people per square mile, the cost of providing public services increases with population." Helen F. Ladd, "Population Growth, Density and the Costs of Providing Public Services," *Urban Studies,* vol. 29, no. 2 (1992), p. 283.

7. Neal R. Peirce, "Maryland's Smart Growth Law: A National Model?" *Washington Post,* April 20, 1997, p. B7.

8. Richard Moe, "Drowning in Sprawl," *Washington Post,* April 20, 1997, p. C8.

9. See the discussion in Frank Ackerman, *Why Do We Recycle? Markets, Values, and Public Policy* (Washington, D.C.: Island Press, 1997), chap. 4.

10. Carol O'Cleireacain, *The Orphaned Capital: Adopting the Right Revenues for the District of Columbia* (Brookings, 1997), chap. 4.

11. Glenn Frankel and Stephen C. Fehr, "As the Economy Grows, the Trees Fall," *Washington Post,* March 23, 1997, p. A20.

12. Timothy Egan, "Urban Sprawl Strains Western States," *New York Times,* December 29, 1996.

13. Water has not been priced correctly in many parts of the West. The federal government, for example, sells water at greatly subsidized rates to California farmers. The underpriced water bloats, among other things, the production of rice, a crop that creates large amounts of methane, a major greenhouse gas. Thomas Gale Moore, *Climate of Fear: Why We Shouldn't Worry about Global Warming* (Washington, D.C.: Cato Institute, 1998), p. 130.

14. Frankel and Fehr, "As the Economy Grows."

15. Joel Garreau makes a similar observation. According to him, low-density suburban settlement may have distinct advantages for the maintenance of ecological diversity. Joel Garreau, *Edge City: Life on the New Frontier* (Doubleday, 1992), pp. 57–58.

16. After the Environmental Protection Agency had expanded, with little statutory basis, the scope of the Clean Water Act to include soil that was dry at the surface but moist within eighteen inches underneath, unwitting farmers or even home gardeners planting flowers on their own "wetlands" might be accused of degrading the environment. See Pietro S. Nivola, "American Social Regulation Meets the Global Economy," in Pietro S. Nivola, ed., *Comparative Disadvantages? Social Regulations and the Global Economy* (Brookings, 1997), p. 22.

17. Peter W. G. Newman and Jeffrey R. Kenworthy, "Gasoline Consumption and Cities: A Comparison of U.S. Cities with a Global Survey," *Journal of the American Planning Association,* vol. 55, no. 1 (Winter 1989), p. 28. The estimate is based on a representative sample of ten major U.S. cities and a dozen European cities. Gasoline usage is for 1980.

18. On a per capita basis, U.S. emissions of CO_2 are more than twice those of Europe. See Marvin S. Soroos, "Preserving the Atmosphere as a Global Commons," *Environment,* vol. 40, no. 2 (March 1998) and World Resources Institute, *World Resources, 1992–93* (Oxford University Press, 1992), pp. 346–47.

19. The reason is simply that the cities gridlock traffic more than do dispersed settings. Peter Gordon and Harry Richardson, "Notes from Underground: The Failure of Urban Mass Transit," *The Public Interest,* no. 94 (Winter 1989), pp. 77–86.

20. Idling, stop-and-go traffic, and slower speeds cause vehicles to spew out more pollutants than when driving at higher speeds. From the standpoint of emissions levels, the length and frequency of suburban vehicular trips may matter less than the degree of road congestion.

21. "Still Worst in U.S., California Air Is at Cleanest Level in 40 Years," *New York Times*, October 31, 1996, p. A20.

22. James Q. Wilson, "Cars and Their Enemies," *Commentary*, July 1997, pp. 20–21.

23. Petroleum, the bulk of which in the United States is used by the transportation sector, accounts for approximately 590 metric tons of carbon emitted into the air each year. Coal is a close second: approximately 500 metric tons per year. U.S. Environmental Protection Agency, *Inventory of Greenhouse Gas Emissions, 1990–1994* (1995), p. A8.

24. Jason Vest and others, "Road Rage," *U.S. News & World Report*, June 2, 1997, p. 28. The official definition of a "congested" road is one where the traffic volume exceeds 80 percent of its designed capacity.

25. The cost of heavy traffic may exceed $75 billion a year, with the Los Angeles area leading the nation at $9 billion annually, followed by New York at $8 billion. Gary S. Becker, "Good-Bye Tollbooths and Traffic Jams?" *Business Week*, May 18, 1998, p. 26. The trouble with such estimates is that, without comparing them to congestion levels under available alternatives, there is no way of knowing whether they represent deadweight losses to the economy.

26. John M. Broder, "Big Social Changes Revive the False God of Numbers," *New York Times*, August 17, 1997, p. E1. On the relative stability of trip durations, and its possible reasons, see Peter Gordon, Harry W. Richardson, and Myung-Jin Jun, "The Commuting Paradox: Evidence from the Top Twenty," *Journal of the American Planning Association*, vol. 57, no. 4 (August 1991), pp. 416–20.

27. "Road Rage," p. 28.

28. Peter Gordon, Ajay Kumar, and Harry Richardson, "The Influence of Metropolitan Spatial Structure on Commuting Times," *Journal of Urban Economics*, vol. 26, no. 2 (September 1989), pp. 138–51. See also, David M. Levinson and Ajay Kumar, "The Rational Locator: Why Travel Times Have Remained Stable," *Journal of the American Planning Association*, vol. 60, no. 3 (Summer 1994), pp. 319–32.

29. For a full discussion of marginal cost pricing of roads see Clifford Winston, "Efficient Transportation Infrastructure Policy," *Journal of Economic Perspectives*, vol. 5, no. 1 (Winter 1991), pp. 113–27.

30. HUD, *The State of the Cities*, p. 38.

31. The figures for these cities are for the years 1979 and 1989. U.S. Bureau of the Census, *City and County Data Book*, 12th ed. (1994).

32. Cities bear a disproportionate burden for poverty-related public expenditures, including police, fire, courts, and general administrative functions. See, for instance, Janet Rothenberg Pack, "Poverty and Urban Public Expenditures," *Urban Studies*, vol. 35, no. 11 (1998), pp. 1995–2019.

33. See Edwin S. Mills and Wallace E. Oates, "The Theory of Local Public Services and Finance: Its Relevance to Urban Fiscal and Zoning Behavior," and Michelle J. White, "Fiscal Zoning in Fragmented Metropolitan Areas," in Edwin S. Mills and Wallace E. Oates, *Fiscal Zoning and Land Use Controls* (D. C. Heath, 1975), chaps. 1 and 3.

34. Andre Donzel, "Regeneration in Marseilles: The Search for Political Stability," in Dennis Judd and Michael Parkinson, eds., *Leadership and Urban Regeneration: Cities in North America and Europe* (London: Sage Publications, 1990), pp. 284–85.

35. See, for example, James Howard Kunstler, *The Geography of Nowhere: The Rise and Decline of America's Man-Made Landscape* (Simon and Schuster, 1993), and, to the right of center, the forum in *American Enterprise*, November/December 1996.

36. Jens S. Dangschat and Jurgen Ossenbrugge, "Hamburg: Crisis Management, Urban Regeneration, and Social Democrats," in Judd and Parkinson, eds., *Leadership and Urban Regeneration*, p. 101.

37. Douglas Lavin, "Tale of Two Job Markets: Why England Works, France Doesn't," *Wall Street Journal*, August 7, 1997, p. A10. The Ministry of the Interior reported that urban violence, fueled by chronic double-digit unemployment and friction with the country's comparatively large urban immigrant population, more than quadrupled nationwide between 1993 and 1997. Craig R. Whitney, "To Burden of Poverty in France, Add Racism," *New York Times,* January 16, 1998.

38. Galia Burgel and Guy Burgel, "Global Trends and City Policies: Friends and Foes of Urban Development?" in Michael A. Cohen, et al., eds., *Preparing for the Urban Future: Global Pressures and Local Forces* (Washington, D.C.: Woodrow Wilson Center, 1996), p. 318.

39. The New York region, defined to include Long Island and northern New Jersey, had a population of 19,738,000 in 1993. The Ile-de-France, roughly corresponding to the urbanized area of metropolitan Paris, had a smaller population: 10,904,000.

40. Economic Planning Agency, Government of Japan, *Economic Survey of Japan (1993–1994): A Challenge to New Frontiers beyond the Severe Adjustment Process* (Tokyo), p. 336. Japan now ought to make domestic spending, not exports, the economy's driving force. A sector badly in need of domestic investment is housing, where there is clearly an unsatisfied demand for more comfortable dwellings. A maze of regulations restricts new building.

41. Government of Japan, Prime Minister's Office, *The National Land Agency* (Tokyo, 1993), pp. 1–6. Although the average building in Tokyo is actually only about three floors high, with so much of Japan's productive capacity concentrated in the region, congestion has reached the point of

interfering with some of Japan's most vaunted industrial practices—just-in-time inventory management, for example.

42. McKinsey Global Institute, *Driving Productivity and Growth in the U.K. Economy* (McKinsey & Co., October 1998), p. 13.

Chapter Five

1. Martin Anderson, "The Federal Bulldozer," in James Q. Wilson, ed., *Urban Renewal: The Record and the Controversy* (MIT Press, 1966), pp. 491–508.

2. Probably the best account of this failed program is Bernard J. Frieden and Marshall Kaplan, *The Politics of Neglect: Urban Aid from Model Cities to Revenue Sharing* (MIT Press, 1975). A lofty objective of the model cities program, Frieden and Kaplan explain, was to slow the process of suburbanization and "bring back" the cities.

3. Ian Mezies, "Boston—An Urban Policy Prototype or a Continuing Urban Policy Problem?" in Marshall Kaplan and Franklin James, eds., *The Future of National Urban Policy* (Duke University Press, 1990), p. 159.

4. Brian J. L. Berry, "Islands of Renewal in Seas of Decay," in Paul E. Peterson, ed., *The New Urban Reality* (Brookings, 1985), pp. 76–77.

5. Bureau of the Census, *County and City Data Book* (1956, 1994).

6. See Timothy Barnekov, Robin Boyle, and Daniel Rich, *Privatism and Urban Policy in Britain and the United States* (Oxford University Press, 1989), pp. 199–206; Marc Bendick Jr. and David W. Rasmussen, "Enterprise Zones and Inner-City Economic Revitalization," in George E. Peterson and Carol W. Lewis, eds., *Reagan and the Cities* (Washington, D.C.: Urban Institute, 1986).

7. One analysis of the results found that, of the 63,300 jobs recorded in the twenty-three zones as of 1986, only 12,900 represented an actual net gain for the economy. The rest were mere transfers and displacements induced by the enterprise-zone incentives. Cited in Anthony Downs, "Contrasting Strategies for the Economic Development of Metropolitan Areas in the United States and Western Europe," in Anita A. Summers, Paul C. Cheshire, and Lanfranco Senn, eds., *Urban Change in the United States and Western Europe: Comparative Analysis and Policy* (Washington, D.C.: Urban Institute), p. 47.

8. Available assessments at this stage do not say whether the business investment and employment in various enterprise zones represents a net addition for the U.S. economy or simply a zero-sum transfer. See, for example, *Activities for Strategic Change: An Overview of Public and Private Investment Activities in the Six Urban Empowerment Zones* (Arlington, Va.: Price Waterhouse, March 1997). What was discovered about the enter-

prise zones of Atlanta is probably true more generally: they "created" few jobs, while mostly relocating them from other sites. See Arthur C. Nelson with Jeffrey H. Migroom, "Regional Growth Management and Central City Vitality: Comparing Development Patterns in Atlanta, Georgia, and Portland, Oregon," in Fritz W. Wagner, Timothy E. Joder, and Anthony J. Mumphrey Jr., eds., *Urban Revitalization: Policies and Programs* (Sage Publications, 1995), p. 16.

9. Robert J. Gibbs, "Urbandizing: A Primer on How Downtowns Can Compete with Retail Malls and Strip Centers," *Planning and Zoning News*, November 1992, pp. 5–9. See also Steven Lagerfeld, "What Main Street Can Learn from the Mall," *Atlantic Monthly*, vol. 276, no. 5 (November 1995), pp. 110–20.

10. Amid the nation's booming economy in the mid-1990s, one might think that cities such as Baltimore would have stabilized their population losses. For all its bold building activity, Baltimore lost another 16,000 residents between June 1996 and July 1997. Brendan K. Koerner, "Cities That Work," *U.S. News & World Report*, June 8, 1998, p. 26.

11. For a comprehensive analysis of these wasteful projects, see Roger G. Noll and Andrew Zimbalist, eds., *Sports, Jobs and Taxes: The Economic Impact of Sports Teams and Stadiums* (Brookings, 1997). See also Mark F. Bernstein, "Sports Stadium Boondoggle," *The Public Interest*, no. 132 (Summer 1998), pp. 45–57. Some similar difficulties attend another favorite urban-planning nostrum: the building of monumental convention centers. Heywood T. Sanders, "Convention Center Follies," *The Public Interest*, no. 132 (Summer 1998), p. 58–72.

12. D.C. Council, Committee on Economic Development, *Report on Barriers to Retail Development in the District of Columbia* (August 1996).

13. Michael E. Porter, "The Competitive Advantage of the Inner City," *Harvard Business Review*, May–June 1995, pp. 55–71.

14. Rochelle L. Stanfield, "City Slickers," *National Journal*, July 19, 1997, pp. 1461–64.

15. Peter Behr, "Barry Seeks Tax Break to Keep Firm in D.C.," *Washington Post*, August 22, 1996, p. D8.

16. Peter Behr, "Northern Virginia Is Still Where the Jobs Are," *Washington Post*, August 31, 1996, p. F1.

17. Jane Bowar, "The Payoffs of Inclusion," *Urban Land*, September 1995, pp. 60–64.

18. William Severini Kowinski, *The Malling of America: An Inside Look at the Great Consumer Paradise* (William Morrow, 1985), p. 317.

19. Despite recent "deregulation," price-fixing remains normal and legal in various segments of the German retail sector. See Greg Steinmetz, "German Consumers Are Seeing Prices Cut in Deregulation Push," *Wall Street Journal*, August 15, 1997. Germany's Federal Cartel Office and the

industry-financed Center for Combating Unfair Competition have taken actions like suing a drugstore that tried to charge $2.15 for a tube of toothpaste instead of the set $2.45, a grocery store that offered discount coupons, and a deli that gave a free cup of coffee to a customer who had already bought ten.

20. "Barbarians at the Check-Out," *The Economist*, October 26, 1996. Kodak Corporation, *Japan: Measures Affecting Photographic Film and Paper,* February 20, 1997, p. 68.

21. David Flath, "Why Are There So Many Retail Stores in Japan?" *Japan and the World Economy,* no. 2 (1990), p. 365.

22. "Excerpts from a Speech by Gingrich about Race," *New York Times,* June 19, 1997.

23. The figures throughout this discussion are for the early 1990s and are tabulated in John Pucher and Christian Lefevre, *The Urban Transport Crisis in Europe and North America* (London: Macmillan Press, 1996), pp. 16–18.

24. James Q. Wilson, "Cars and Their Enemies," *Commentary,* July 1997, p. 21.

25. A study that compared preapproval costs and ridership estimates of eight urban rail projects built in the 1970s and 1980s found that only Washington's Metrorail system acquired ridership anywhere near the forecasted level. Don K. Pickrell, "A Desire Named Streetcar: Fantasy and Fact in Rail Transit Planning," *Journal of the American Planning Association,* vol. 58 (Spring 1992), p. 169. Some new light-rail lines, such as one recently opened in St. Louis, have recorded significantly more riders than originally predicted. But operating losses borne by the local authorities have often been much higher than expected as well. Fares on the St. Louis system, for example, only recover 27.7 percent of operating costs. The figure for Baltimore's system has been 25 percent recovered, and for that of Los Angeles, 15.6 percent. Eliza Newlin Carney, "A Desire Named Streetcar," *Governing,* February 1994, pp. 36–39.

26. As early as 1921, automobile ownership in California was nearly double the U.S. average. The unchecked horizontal growth of Los Angeles, though obviously assisted by mass motorization, got underway even before it, thanks in part to the far-flung reach of the city's streetcar lines. James J. Flink, *The Automobile Age* (MIT Press, 1988), pp. 140, 142.

27. See Constance E. Beaumont, *How Superstore Sprawl Can Harm Communities and What Citizens Can Do About It* (Washington, D.C.: National Trust for Historic Preservation, 1994), p. 3.

28. The bizarre decision of planners in Los Angeles to build a twenty-two-mile subway line in one of the world's least densely settled urban centers has come to be known as the "subway from hell." William Claiborne,

"L.A. Subway Tests Mass Transit's Limits," *Washington Post,* June 10, 1998, pp. A1, A8. Los Angeles County has earmarked a phenomenal $78.2 billion for the region's "Thirty-Year Integrated Transportation Plan." Peter Gordon and Harry W. Richardson, "Beyond Polycentricity: The Dispersed Metropolis, Los Angeles, 1970–1990," *Journal of the American Planning Association,* vol. 62, no. 3 (Summer 1996), p. 292.

29. Since 1970, more than a dozen state governments have established comprehensive growth-managing programs on a statewide basis or for subareas.

30. Stephen C. Fehr, "Montgomery's Line of Defense against the Suburban Invasion," *Washington Post,* March 25, 1997. Of the top ten counties in the United States that effectively preserve farmland, seven are in Maryland. No other urban county in the nation has managed to protect as much green space—93,252 acres as of 1996—as has Montgomery County.

31. Timothy Egan, "Drawing a Hard Line against Urban Sprawl," *New York Times,* December 30, 1996.

32. William Claiborne, "Cracks in Portland's 'Great Wall,'" *Washington Post,* September 29, 1997, p. A1.

33. Alan Ehrenhalt, "The Great Wall of Portland," *Governing,* vol. 10 (May 1997).

34. Claiborne, "Cracks in Portland's 'Great Wall.'"

35. Ehrenhalt, "The Great Wall."

36. David Rusk, "A Look at Segregation and Poverty: How We Promote Poverty," *Washington Post,* May 18, 1997, p. C1.

37. See William A. Fischel, *Do Growth Controls Matter?* (Cambridge, Mass.: Lincoln Institute of Land Policy, May 1990). S. I. Schwartz, D. E. Hansen, and R. Green, "Suburban Growth Controls and the Price of New Housing," *Journal of Environmental Economics and Management,* vol. 8 (December 1981), pp. 303–20. Lawrence Katz and Kenneth Rosen, "Interjurisdictional Effects of Growth Controls on Housing Prices," *Journal of Law and Economics,* vol. 30, no. 1 (April 1987), pp. 149–60.

38. Fehr, "Montgomery's Line of Defense."

39. Downs, "Contrasting Strategies," p. 19.

40. Since 1970, smog in the United States has diminished by almost a third, even though the number of cars, servicing a sprawling style of urban development, has nearly doubled. Gregg Easterbrook, "Greenhouse Common Sense," *U.S. News & World Report,* December 1, 1997, p. 58. On alternative spatial development patterns and the likely effects on pollution abatement, see Robert W. Bruchell and others, *Impact Assessment of the New Jersey Interim State Development and Redevelopment Plan* (Trenton: New Jersey Office of State Planning, 1992), but see also Brian J. L. Berry and others, *Land Use, Urban Form and Environmental Quality* (University of Chicago,

1974), p. 426. Berry and his co-researchers concluded that air quality would be improved in Hartford, Chicago, and Seattle by "corridor" development rather than sprawl.

41. Anthony Downs, *Stuck in Traffic: Coping with Peak-Hour Traffic Congestion* (Brookings, 1992), p. 80.

42. *American Farmland*, no. 3, vol. 17 (Fall 1996).

43. So far, only about one-quarter of the American states have enacted statewide growth management legislation. As of 1993, this group, mostly concentrated along the coasts, included only one of the states (Florida) with a population exceeding ten million. Several of the state programs—including those of Maine, Vermont, and Rhode Island—authorized during the 1970s and 1980s are now, in Alan Altshuler words, "in virtual hibernation." And prospects appear to have dimmed for the adoption of new programs in major states, such as California, where interest ran high in the late 1980s. For a critical summary of the situation, see Altshuler, "The Ideo-Logics of Urban Land Use Politics," in Martha A. Derthick, ed., *Dilemmas of Scale in America's Federal Democracy* (Cambridge University Press and Woodrow Wilson Center Press, forthcoming).

44. David Rusk, *Cities without Suburbs* (Johns Hopkins University Press, 1993), p. 10.

45. Rusk, *Cities without Suburbs*, pp. 43–45.

46. The assumption that unitary "metro" governments deliver services evenly among the incorporated communities and neighborhoods is just that—an assumption. There are substantial neighborhood disparities in the levels of services even within existing municipal governments. For a detailed case study, see Pietro S. Nivola, *The Urban Service Problem* (D.C. Heath, 1979).

47. The classic exposition of this thesis is Charles M. Tiebout, "A Pure Theory of Local Expenditures," *Journal of Political Economy,* vol. 64 (October 1956).

48. See, more generally, Edward C. Banfield and Morton Grodzins, *Government and Housing in Metropolitan Areas* (McGraw-Hill, 1958), p. 37.

49. Timothy Egan, "Drawing a Hard Line against Urban Sprawl," *New York Times,* December 30, 1996.

Chapter Six

1. Further, if the Joneses eventually sell their property, their capital gain can be rolled over, permitting the purchase of an even larger house.

2. For a complete discussion of these ideas, see M. Jeff Hamond, *Tax Waste, Not Work: How Changing What We Tax Can Lead to a Stronger Economy and a Cleaner Environment* (San Francisco: Redefining Progress, April 1997).

3. John Carey, "Give Green Taxes a Green Light," *Business Week,* April 13, 1998, p. 31.

4. Needless to say, a significant levy per ton on carbon would not be painless. Its macroeconomic perturbations, however, could be offset over the long term by reductions in other taxes, such as the impost on payrolls. For an analysis of the optimal carbon tax, see William D. Nordhaus, *Managing the Global Commons: The Economics of Climate Change* (MIT Press, 1994), especially pp. 184–86, 208–09.

5. Studies based on the energy price increases between 1973 and 1980, adjusted for growth in real incomes, suggest that increased automotive commuting costs of that magnitude would likely slow decentralization "somewhat," although hardly enough to reverse it. See, for instance, Richard F. Muth, "Energy Prices and Urban Decentralization," in Anthony Downs and Katherine L. Bradbury, eds., *Energy Costs, Urban Development and Housing* (Brookings, 1984), p. 99.

6. Plenty of horror stories can be told about unsound road projects, but a notable one was the completion of Interstate 90 near Seattle in 1991, at the time the most costly seven-mile stretch of road built in the United States. The eight-lane behemoth cut through the forest east of Lake Washington and encouraged development in the Cascade foothills.

7. Quoted in William Plowden, *The Motor Car and Politics, 1896–1970* (London: The Bodley Head, 1971), 190–91.

8. See James A. Dunn Jr., "The Politics of Motor Fuel Taxes and Infrastructure Funds in France and the United States," *Policy Studies Journal,* vol. 21 (Summer 1993), pp. 271–84. By 1981 the *Fond,* which had survived in name only, was formally absorbed into the *Budget général de l'état.* Conseil economique et social, *Les droits d'accise* (Paris, 1991), p. 108.

9. See Pietro S. Nivola and Robert W. Crandall, *The Extra Mile: Rethinking Energy Policy for Automotive Transportation* (Brookings, 1995), pp. 75–76.

10. Trust fund revenues come from an 18.3 cents per gallon tax on gasoline, of which 15.45 cents is for highways and 2.85 cents for transit. Prior to the 1993 budget agreements, the gas tax stood at 14 cents. The 4.3-cent increment enacted that year had been intended for budget-balancing. Instead, it found its way to the trust's coffers and quickly became a windfall for the House Transportation and Infrastructure Committee. Aware of the danger, in 1997 Representative John Kasich (R-Ohio), chairman of the House Budget Committee, and Senator Connie Mack (R-Fla.) introduced legislation that would have nearly eliminated the entire federal gasoline tax, leaving just 2 cents for highways. State governments would have been left to decide for themselves whether to raise state taxes to pay for their additional roads. The Kasich-Mack bill would have prevented any subsequent "abomination" (Kasich's word) such as the transportation bill that

emerged in 1998. Short of the Kasich-Mack proposal's bold step, even stripping just the 4.3 cents supplement from the current federal tax would have helped cut the bill down to size.

11. Additional improvements in traffic management are badly needed. Among them is an end to the folly of subsidized parking facilities. See Peter Gordon and Harry Richardson, "Notes from Underground: The Failure of Urban Mass Transit," *The Public Interest*, no. 94 (Winter 1989), p. 86.

12. Pricing incentives are being tried here and there. On the Riverside Freeway east of Los Angeles and on parts of I-15 near San Diego, for instance, "HO/T (high occupancy/toll) lanes" have been created and seem to work well. During rush hours, these lanes are used either free of charge by carpoolers or for a toll charge (collected electronically) by autos with only one or two occupants. What is striking, however, is how slowly such commonsense innovations are being implemented around the country.

13. Nationwide, homicides declined by another 9 percent in the first half of 1997, and violent crime overall was down by 5 percent. Roberto Suro, "Drop in Murder Rate Accelerates in Cities," *Washington Post*, December 31, 1997, p. A1.

14. A survey of businesses in Atlanta found employers citing break-ins, theft, and extra insurance and security costs as their three biggest problems. Cited in Michael E. Porter, "New Strategies for Inner-City Economic Development," *Economic Development Quarterly*, February 1997, p. 19. Such findings come as no surprise. At the end of 1993 the overall costs of crime in the United States were estimated to be a stunning $425 billion each year. Since the bulk of the problem lies in and around the core of metropolitan areas, city businesses, households, and treasuries bear the brunt of crime's colossal costs. Michael J. Mandel and others, "The Economics of Crime," *Business Week*, December 13, 1993, p. 72.

15. Michael Powell, "Showing Dubious Progress in a Deadly District," *Washington Post*, April 19, 1998, p. A22.

16. A new generation of street criminals is coming of age, possibly "the youngest, biggest, and baddest generation any society has ever known," write William J. Bennett, John J. DiIulio Jr., and John P. Walters in *Body Count: Moral Poverty and How to Win America's War against Crime and Drugs* (Simon and Schuster, 1996).

17. See John J. DiIulio Jr., "Rule of Law: Abolish the Death Penalty, Officially," *Wall Street Journal*, December 15, 1997.

18. Jerome H. Skolnick, "Tough Guys," *American Prospect*, January–February, 1997, p. 87. See also Stephen Glass, "Anatomy of a Policy Fraud," *New Republic*, November 17, 1997, pp. 22–25.

19. The effective form of community policing seems to be the type that extends beyond traditional law enforcement. Despite the recent decline

in crime rates, *fear* of crime remains high. In part, this may be because outward signs of social disorder—burnt-out or dilapidated buildings, piles of trash, abandoned cars, graffiti, aggressive panhandlers, and so on— keep reaffirming a perception that criminal activity lurks in the neighborhood. Consequently, municipal authorities that dedicate significant time and resources not only to making arrests but to maintaining a semblance of public order, including visual manifestations, may allay the local sense of foreboding that sometimes drives as many people away from the cities as do the actual crime statistics. For a full discussion of these issues see James Q. Wilson and George L. Kelling, "Broken Windows," *Atlantic Monthly,* March 1982; James Q. Wilson and George L. Kelling, "Making Neighborhoods Safe," *Atlantic Monthly,* February 1989; and George L. Kelling and Catherine M. Coles, *Fixing Broken Windows* (Free Press, 1996).

20. For a superb analysis of this process see Powell, "Showing Dubious Progress," p. A22.

21. The Chicago Housing Authority has recently demolished ten high-rise public housing buildings and plans to knock down twenty more. Residents are being relocated to mixed-income developments and private housing. "High-Rise Brought Low at Last," *The Economist,* July 11, 1998, p. 31. As of 1997, the Clinton administration had funded the demolition of 46,000 public housing units nationwide. See Howard Husock, "Public Housing as a 'Poorhouse,'" *Public Interest,* no. 129 (Fall 1997), p. 74. An alternative to demolition in some cases is to diversify the income range of public housing tenants. Mixed-income projects are preferable to ghetto-like conditions. New legislation in Congress is finally moving in this direction.

22. The legislation added 50,000 new rent vouchers for families searching for private apartments and eliminated a penny-wise budgetary measure that would have slashed another 30,000 to 40,000 vouchers out of a 1.1 million annual total. Judith Havemann, "Hill Sets Changes for Public Housing," *Washington Post,* October 6, 1998, p. A4.

23. Needless to say, it is an open question whether government is capable of formulating a coherent and humane agenda, as opposed to a new hash of intrusive prohibitions, punishments, and pontifications. Advocates of a newly paternalistic role for "the state" ought to worry about inviting it to promote "family values," whether socially engineered by agitators of the Left or Right. Still, it is not clear why government should be in the business of subsidizing day care facilities but not mothers who wish to raise their children at home, or taxing married couples more onerously than singles, or levying a heavy payroll tax on working households but nothing comparable on millionaires collecting social security, and so forth.

24. As David Popenoe notes, America's "marital breakup rate is by far the highest among the advanced societies. . . . The chances of a first marriage ending in divorce in America today are about one in two." The

percentage of single-parent families also ranks highest. David Popenoe, *Disturbing the Nest: Family Change and Decline in Modern Societies* (New York: Aldine de Gruyter, 1988), p. 287. Formal divorce rates may understate the frequency of family breakup. Counting separations, by some estimates as many as *two-thirds* of all recent marriages eventually collapse in the United States. See William J. Goode, *The World Changes in Divorce Patterns* (Yale University Press, 1993), p. 153.

25. The divorce rate in Japan as of 1992 was less than one-third that of the United States. When mothers of teenagers were asked, in a comparative survey, whether they believed "a man and a wife, even if they want a divorce, should consider their children's future and remain married," almost three-quarters of those in Japan said they should stay married. Nearly two-thirds of those in the United States favored the option of divorce. See Seymour Martin Lipset, *American Exceptionalism: A Double-Edged Sword* (W. W. Norton, 1996), p. 229. For those who impute social disorder to income inequality, it may be noted that family decomposition helps explain a substantial share of the increase in inequality in the United States since 1979. See Gary Burtless, "Effects of Growing Wage Disparities and Changing Family Composition on the U.S. Income Distribution," paper prepared for the European Economic Association Meeting, Berlin, September 2–5, 1998.

26. The United States spends more than $300 billion a year on its public schools—5.6 percent of GNP. The cost of education, adjusted for inflation, rose by 50 percent between 1974 and 1991. See Paul E. Peterson, "School Choice: A Report Card," in Paul E. Peterson and Bryan C. Hassel, eds., *Learning from School Choice* (Brookings, 1998), pp. 3, 9.

27. Although private scholarship programs serving more than 13,000 students now exist in more than thirty cities, state-funded choice programs that give eligible families an opportunity to choose their schools currently exist in only two cities, Milwaukee and Cleveland. Considerable controversy has surrounded the results of the Milwaukee experiment. See Daniel McGroarty, "School Choice Slandered," *The Public Interest*, Fall 1994, pp. 94–111. Paul E. Peterson and his colleagues recently found that choice students in Milwaukee showed significant academic gains after three or four years in the program. Peterson, "School Choice," p. 22. Still, it is hard to draw broad inferences about the efficacy of school choice from this isolated case. Hampering more generalized research regarding participation in choice projects is the fact that most of the projects conducted thus far have not constituted randomized experiments.

28. See, in general, Paul T. Hill and Mary Beth Celio, *Fixing Urban Schools* (Brookings, 1998), esp. pp. 22, 54–57. There is another, perhaps more intractable phenomenon that can frustrate informed choice: ram-

pant grade inflation, as competing schools come to fear that issuing unsatisfactory grades may offend customers. This tendency already appears to afflict the most competitive sector of the U.S. educational system: institutions of higher education.

29. Department of Education, National Center for Education Statistics, *Historical Trends, 1969 to 1989*, pp. 38–39; U.S. Department of Education, National Center for Education Statistics, *Digest of Education Statistics, 1997*, p. 76.

30. Some of the nation's worst school systems have especially low pupil-teacher ratios. The District of Columbia's ratio, for example, is 14.2 pupils per teacher—the fourth lowest among all states. National Education Association, "Pupil/Teacher Ratio, 1995 and Expenditures per ADA, 1995–96: All States," *Ed-Data* (Palo Alto, Calif.: EdSource, Inc., 1997). See also Eric A. Hanushek, "The Economics of Schooling: Production and Efficiency in Public Schools," *Journal of Economic Literature*, vol. 24 (September 1986), p. 1167.

31. According to the U.S. Department of Education, big-city school systems spent more than $5,447 per pupil in 1989–90, compared with $5,427 in suburban districts and $4,507 in rural ones. Peterson, "School Choice," p. 12. For a sobering general review of whether school resources make a difference in educational performances, see Eric A. Hanushek, "School Resources and Student Performance," in Gary Burtless, ed., *Does Money Matter? The Effects of School Resources on Student Achievement and Adult Success* (Brookings, 1996), pp. 43–73. For a contrasting assessment, see Larry V. Hedges and Rob Greenwald, "Have Times Changed? Relation between School Resources and Student Performance," in Burtless, *Does Money Matter?* pp. 74–92.

32. Charles Cobb, "D.C.'s Top-Down Troubles: The City Has the Means to Be Great. Why Can't Its Leaders Fix What's Wrong?" *Washington Post*, April 26, 1998, p. C5.

33. Rene Sanchez, "Urban Students Not Making the Mark," *Washington Post*, January 8, 1998.

34. In a major nationwide survey, Terry Moe of Stanford University found 79 percent of poor inner-city respondents favoring a "voucher plan"—61 percent favoring such a plan "strongly." See Paul E. Peterson and Jay P. Greene, "Race Relations and Central City Schools: It's Time for an Experiment with Vouchers," *Brookings Review*, Spring 1998, pp. 34–35.

35. "Italian Small Businesses: Change in the Heartland," *The Economist*, April 2, 1994, p. 63. There are still more shopkeepers per capita in Italy than in any other western country except Portugal and Greece. "Open Up," *The Economist*, March 14, 1998, p. 59.

36. For a nuanced analysis of labor market rigidities in Europe and the United States, see Stephen Nickell, "Unemployment and Labor Market

Rigidities: Europe versus North America," *Journal of Economic Perspectives,* vol. 11, no. 3 (Summer 1997), pp. 55–74.

37. Zoning ordinances, typically separating commercial from residential areas, have increased the domination of large stores. For a broad comparative analysis with Japan, see David Flath, "Why Are There So Many Retail Stores in Japan,"*Japan and the World Economy,* no. 2 (1990), especially pp. 366, 382–83. See also George W. Liebmann, "Modernization of Zoning: A Means to Reform," *Regulation,* vol. 19, no. 2 (1996). Allowance for mixed land uses has been one of the regulatory changes that has helped revive a number of old urban neighborhoods. For an account of this "SoHo syndrome," see Roberta Brandes Gratz, *Cities Back from the Edge: New Life for Downtown* (John Wiley, 1998), chap. 13.

38. For a full treatment of this subject, in comparative perspective, see Pietro S. Nivola, "American Social Regulation Meets the Global Economy," in Pietro S. Nivola, ed., *Comparative Disadvantages? Social Regulations and the Global Economy* (Brookings, 1997), chap. 2.

39. See Walter K. Olson, *The Excuse Factory: How Employment Law is Paralyzing the American Workplace* (Free Press, 1997).

40. On these issues, see Pietro S. Nivola, "The New Pork Barrel," *The Public Interest,* no. 131 (Spring 1998), pp. 92–104.

41. McDonald's Corporation had begun placing warning labels on its coffee cups in 1991. Yet three years later a jury ordered it to pay $2.9 million to a woman who scalded herself by spilling coffee on her lap. The case, far from being a fluke, set off a rash of similar suits against other eating places, some of which have taken to supplementing the warnings on cups by training employees to tell customers how to drink the contents carefully. Cindy Webb, "Boiling Mad," *Business Week,* August 21, 1995, p. 32.

42. Pascal Zachary, "Korean Grocer Learns the Law Doesn't Care about His Good Deeds," *Wall Street Journal,* July 30, 1996, p. A1.

43. Susan Diesenhouse, "Housing Investment Surges in Cambridge: End of Rent Control Brings on Upgrades and New Construction," *New York Times,* December 14, 1997, p. 51.

44. "Going Beyond City Limits?" *Business Week,* July 7, 1997, p. 98.

45. The empirical research on this point is extensive, but see, for example, B. Peter Pashigian, "The Effect of Environmental Regulation on Optimal Plant Size and Factor Shares," *Journal of Law and Economics,* vol. 27, no. 1 (April 1984), pp. 1–28; Ann P. Bartel and Lacy Glenn Thomas, "Predation through Regulation: The Wage and Profit Effects of the Occupational Safety and Health Administration and the Environmental Protection Agency," *Journal of Law and Economics,* vol. 30, no. 2 (October 1987), pp. 239–64; Ann P. Bartel and Lacy Glenn Thomas, "Direct and Indirect Effects of Regulation: A New Look at OSHA's Impact," *Journal of Law and Economics,* vol. 28, no. 1 (April 1985), pp. 1–25.

46. Less than one-third of all local government income in Germany derives from local revenues. Manfred Konukiewitz and Hellmut Wollman, "Physical Planning in a Federal System: The Case of West Germany," in David H. McKay, ed., *Planning and Politics in Western Europe* (St. Martin's Press, 1982), p. 75. Two-thirds of the income of urban governments in the United States comes from local revenue sources. See Dennis R. Judd, *The Politics of American Cities: Private Power and Public Policy*, 3d ed. (Scott, Foresman, 1988), p. 201.

47. The so-called Unfunded Mandates Reform Act of 1995 has barely begun to address the extent of the problem. See U.S. General Accounting Office, *Unfunded Mandates: Reform Act Has Had Little Effect on Agencies' Rulemaking Actions* (February 1998).

48. The statist systems in England, France, Italy, or Holland impose plenty of standards, but their costs appear to be much more fully reimbursed. Local governments in Italy and the Netherlands, for example, raise only about 10 percent of their budgets locally. For a wide range of local services—including educational institutions, hospitals, prisons, courts, utilities, and so on—the central government funds 80 percent of the expense to England's local councils. "Local Difficulties," *The Economist*, May 9, 1998, pp. 55–56.

49. Among the largely unfunded mandates bearing down on local school systems are the federal special-education program, requirements for gender-role discrimination education, asbestos removal, school recycling, safe drinking water tests, and so on. Gregory A. Fossedal, "Help for Schools? Try Deregulation," *Wall Street Journal*, March 27, 1996, p. A22.

50. See United States Advisory Commission on Intergovernmental Relations, *The Role of Federal Mandates in Intergovernmental Relations* (ACIR, January 1996). On average, special education costs up to $14,000 per pupil, more than twice the regular per pupil cost. As our delineation of learning disabilities expanded, the share of students qualifying for special education reached 12 percent in 1995, up from 9 percent in 1977. Fossedal, "Help for Schools?" p. A22.

51. In some big cities the federal reimbursement has been half that much. In fiscal 1980, for instance, New York City received $8.5 million in federal aid while spending an estimated $221 million in tax-levy dollars for special education. Edward I. Koch, "The Mandate Millstone," *The Public Interest*, no. 61 (Fall 1980), p. 47. Nationally, between 1967 and 1991, special education claimed a substantially larger share of all new expenditures on education than did other programs of educational support. Edward A. Zelinsky, "The Unsolved Problem of the Unfunded Mandate," *Ohio Northern University Law Review*, vol. 23, no. 3 (1997), p. 760.

52. Doug Struck, "Special Ed System Exacts a Price in Waste, Neglect," *Washington Post*, February 19, 1997, p. A1.

53. Koch, "Mandate Millstone," p. 45.

54. Koch, "Mandate Millstone," p. 45. Nobody suggests that special provisions for persons with disabilities should be denied. But some means of providing access are expensive, and if the federal government insists on requiring these costly options, it should pay for them.

55. For a full account of the pre-ADA disability mandates and their revisions, see Robert A. Katzmann, *Institutional Disability: The Saga of Transportation Policy for the Disabled* (Brookings, 1986), especially pp. 123–25. Even though the Washington Metro—the nation's most modern and well-designed subway system—is increasingly hard pressed to fund its growing maintenance bill (estimated at $200 million a year), the system will be required to tear up forty-five stations and install bumpy tiles along platform edges, at an estimated cost of more than $15 million. Alice Reid, "Safety Effort to Cost Metro $15 Million," *Washington Post*, November 14, 1997, p. B3. Of course, this added expense will not fall exclusively on the District of Columbia. The transit authority in Washington, as in many metropolitan areas, is a regional entity, whose revenues are collected on an areawide basis. However, each jurisdiction has to make a contribution—and the District is not in a particularly strong financial position to incur transit-system surcharges.

56. In 1980 all federal and state mandated programs combined were apparently extracting from New York City an estimated total of $415 million annually, according to Koch's numbers in "Mandate Millstone," p. 42.

57. Report from City Administrative Officer, "Impact of Federal and State Unfunded Mandates and Recommendations for Action," City of Los Angeles, June 17, 1994, p. 1.

58. Los Angeles's total revenue receipts in 1997–98 were slightly more than $4 billion. City of Los Angeles, *1997–98 Budget Summary*.

59. See Pietro S. Nivola, "Gridlocked or Gaining Ground? U.S. Regulatory Reform in the Energy Sector," *Brookings Review*, vol. 11, no. 3 (Summer 1993), pp. 36–41.

60. For a comprehensive analysis of the CAFE programs and its rational alternatives, see Nivola and Crandall, *The Extra Mile*.

61. Between October and mid-March 1998, the price of crude oil plunged from $22 a barrel to a low of $12.91. Gary McWilliams, "Living in a World of Cheap Oil," *Business Week*, March 30, 1998, p. 30.

62. An average tax rate closer to Canada's than to Europe's would undoubtedly be considered more appropriate for the United States. In any case, we estimate that even a 25-cents-per-gallon boost in the gasoline tax— a moderate increase compared to European levels—would have saved as much oil as did the CAFE standards from their inception, but at a fraction of the social cost. See Nivola and Crandall, *The Extra Mile*, p. 112.

63. The CAFE system sets separate fuel-economy targets for passenger cars (27.5 mpg) and for light trucks (20.7). With vans, sport utility vehicles, and pickups now composing almost half the market, the dual standard obviously creates a gigantic loophole—one that would not exist if a higher gasoline tax simply replaced the regulations. As things stand, vehicles such as the Chevrolet Tahoe score 14 miles per gallon (mpg) in city driving. The Toyota Land Cruiser gets 13 mpg, the Dodge Ram 2500 pickup gets 11 mpg, and so on. Warren Brown, "Driven to Excess," *Washington Post*, May 4, 1996.

64. On labor market effects, see George J. Borjas, Richard B. Freeman, and Lawrence F. Katz, "How Much Do Immigration and Trade Affect Labor Market Outcomes?" *Brookings Papers on Economic Activity*, vol. 1 (1997), especially pp. 4–10. But see also Susan M. Collins, "Economic Integration and the American Worker: An Overview," in Susan M. Collins, ed., *Imports, Exports, and the American Worker* (Brookings, 1998), p. 8.

65. For an upbeat assessment, see Stephen Moore, *A Fiscal Portrait of the Newest Americans* (Washington, D.C.: National Immigration Forum and Cato Institute, July 1998). A recent study by Madeline Zavodny of the Federal Reserve Bank of Atlanta found little evidence that new immigrants choose locations based on welfare benefits. "Do Immigrants Chase Benefits?" *Business Week*, December 1, 1997, p. 28. On the daunting methodological complexities of estimating net fiscal impacts, see Barry Edmonston and Ronald Lee, eds., *Local Fiscal Effects of Illegal Immigration: Report of a Workshop* (Washington, D.C.: National Academy Press for the National Research Council, 1996).

66. Kristin F. Butcher and Anne Morrison Piehl, *Recent Immigrants: Unexpected Implications for Crime and Incarceration* (Cambridge, Mass.: National Bureau of Economic Research, Working Paper No. 6067, June, 1997), p. 34. Interestingly, some researchers have found similar differentials in academic conduct. Ruben G. Rumbaut of Michigan State University found, for example, that the most disciplined, hardest working, and respectful students "tend to be the most recently arrived." As Rumbaut explains, they are the ones "who have not been here long enough to be Americanized into bad habits, into a Beavis and Butt-head perspective of the world." See William Branigin, "Immigrants Question Idea of Assimilation," *Washington Post*, May 25, 1998, p. A13.

67. Branigin, "Immigrants Question Idea of Assimilation," p. A13. More generally, in the 1980s cities with high levels of immigration appeared to record more job creation and higher average incomes, along with lower poverty rates and often less crime. Stephen Moore, "New Blood for Cities," *American Enterprise*, September/October 1997, pp. 12–13.

68. Blaine Harden and Jay Mathews, "New Mix Enlivens N.Y. Melting Pot," *Washington Post,* May 26, 1997, pp. A1, A14. Christina Duff, "Most of the Nation's Ten Largest Cities Retain Crowns, Thanks to Immigration," *Wall Street Journal,* November 19, 1997, p. A6.

69. Joel Kotkin, *Can the Cities Be Saved?* (Milken Institute, 1997).

70. The figure is in "Trouble in Paradise," *The Economist,* March 14, 1998, p. 3.

71. Peter Skerry and Stephen J. Rockwell, "The Cost of a Tighter Border: People-Smuggling Networks," *Los Angeles Times,* May 3, 1998.

72. On this mixed bag, see Mark J. Miller, "Employer Sanctions in France: From the Campaign against Illegal Alien Employment to the Campaign against Illegal Work," in U.S. Commission on Immigration Reform, *Curbing Unlawful Migration* (1997), pp. 605–30.

73. Anne Swardson, "France Watches Warily as Violent Protests Mount," *Washington Post,* January 3, 1998, p. A15.

Chapter Seven

1. Phillip J. Longman, "Who Pays for Sprawl?" *U.S. News & World Report,* April 27, 1998, p. 22.

Index

Printed in the United States
120569LV00004B/340-429/A